THE "NEW IMPERIALISM"

Analysis of Late Nineteenth-Century Expansion

PROBLEMS IN EUROPEAN CIVILIZATION

UNDER THE EDITORIAL DIRECTION OF

Ralph W. Greenlaw* and Dwight E. Lee†

DECLINE AND FALL OF THE ROMAN EMPIRE — WHY DID IT COLLAPSE? †

THE PIRENNE THESIS — ANALYSIS, CRITICISM, AND REVISION*

THE CORONATION OF CHARLEMAGNE — WHAT DID IT SIGNIFY? *

THE GREGORIAN EPOCH — REFORMATION, REVOLUTION, REACTION? *

INNOCENT III — VICAR OF CHRIST OR LORD OF THE WORLD? †

THE RENAISSANCE — MEDIEVAL OR MODERN? *

MACHIAVELLI — CYNIC, PATRIOT, OR POLITICAL SCIENTIST? *

THE REFORMATION — MATERIAL OR SPIRITUAL? *

THE CHARACTER OF PHILIP II — THE PROBLEM OF MORAL JUDGMENTS IN HISTORY*

PROTESTANTISM AND CAPITALISM — THE WEBER THESIS AND ITS CRITICS*

THE ORIGINS OF THE ENGLISH CIVIL WAR — CONSPIRACY, CRUSADE, OR CLASS CONFLICT? *

THE REVOLUTION OF 1688 — WHIG TRIUMPH OR PALACE REVOLUTION? †

PETER THE GREAT — REFORMER OR REVOLUTIONARY? †

THE GREATNESS OF LOUIS XIV — MYTH OR REALITY? *

THE EIGHTEENTH-CENTURY REVOLUTION — FRENCH OR WESTERN? †

THE ECONOMIC ORIGINS OF THE FRENCH REVOLUTION — POVERTY OR PROSPERITY? *

METTERNICH, THE "COACHMAN OF EUROPE" — STATESMAN OR EVIL GENIUS? *

THE INDUSTRIAL REVOLUTION IN BRITAIN — TRIUMPH OR DISASTER? *

1848 — A TURNING POINT? *

NAPOLEON III — BUFFOON, MODERN DICTATOR, OR SPHINX? †

OTTO VON BISMARCK — A HISTORICAL ASSESSMENT*

THE "NEW IMPERIALISM" — ANALYSIS OF LATE NINETEENTH-CENTURY EXPANSION*

THE DREYFUS AFFAIR — TRAGEDY OF ERRORS? †

THE OUTBREAK OF THE FIRST WORLD WAR — WHO WAS RESPONSIBLE? *

THE RUSSIAN REVOLUTION AND BOLSHEVIK VICTORY — WHY AND HOW? *

THE VERSAILLES SETTLEMENT — WAS IT FOREDOOMED TO FAILURE? *

THE ETHIOPIAN CRISIS — TOUCHSTONE OF APPEASEMENT? *

THE NAZI REVOLUTION — GERMANY'S GUILT OR GERMANY'S FATE? *

THE BRITISH IN INDIA — IMPERIALISM OR TRUSTEESHIP? †

THE OUTBREAK OF THE SECOND WORLD WAR — DESIGN OR BLUNDER? †

THE COLD WAR — IDEOLOGICAL CONFLICT OR POWER STRUGGLE? †

Other volumes in preparation

PROBLEMS IN EUROPEAN CIVILIZATION

THE "NEW IMPERIALISM"

Analysis of
Late Nineteenth-Century Expansion

EDITED WITH AN INTRODUCTION BY

Harrison M. Wright, SWARTHMORE COLLEGE

D. C. HEATH AND COMPANY · BOSTON

Table of Contents

J. HOLLAND ROSE
Three Conditions of Expansion I

J. A. HOBSON
Imperialism. A Study 4

V. I. LENIN
The Highest Stage of Capitalism 29

LEONARD WOOLF
Empire and Commerce 39

JOSEPH A. SCHUMPETER
Imperialism as a Social Atavism 47

MURRAY GREENE
Schumpeter's Imperialism — A Critical Note 62

WILLIAM L. LANGER
A Critique of Imperialism 68

EUGENE STALEY
Foreign Investment and Foreign Expansion 77

CARLTON J. H. HAYES

Bases of a New National Imperialism   81

NICHOLAS MANSERGH

Diplomatic Reasons for Expansion   89

PIERRE RENOUVIN

The Politics of Imperialist Expansion   96

HANNAH ARENDT

The Alliance Between Mob and Capital   101

Suggestions for Additional Reading   107

Introduction

DURING the first two thirds of the nineteenth century the interest of European states in overseas expansion reached its lowest point in several centuries. The age of colonial empire-building seemed at last to have come to an end. By 1800 France had already lost most of her old empire and Great Britain had had to give up the thirteen American colonies. In the decades following, Spain and Portugal lost their South American possessions. The still-divided Germany made no attempt to acquire territories, nor did the various Italian states. Of all the continental powers only France undertook any serious overseas ventures for fifty years after the Napoleonic Wars; and while she embroiled herself in several areas (Algeria, Tahiti, Cochin China), her haphazard interest and the small gains that resulted were in no way comparable to her activities in centuries past. Great Britain, to be sure, acquired large territories in the mid-nineteenth century (such as New Zealand, the Punjab, central Canada, western Australia), but most of this gain was contiguous to areas already occupied and — except in India — settled by British colonists who were at the same time being granted almost unheard-of political freedoms. The grants of "responsible government," the final repeal of the Navigation Acts and of the Corn Laws, and the rising tide of free trade were signs that a substantial body of opinion in mid-nineteenth-century Britain felt the old colonial policies had been neither justifiable nor worth while. In spite of the increasingly vigorous activities of traders, missionaries, and explorers, the general sentiment throughout Europe by 1850 was running against any extensive political commitments overseas.

But this period of relative disinterest did not last out the century. Suddenly, and almost simultaneously, between 1870 and 1900, the states of Europe began to extend their control over vast areas of the world. Britain had the largest empire to start with and in the end acquired most new territory. But France, Germany, Belgium, Portugal, Italy, and others also made extensive gains. It has been estimated that the Europeans expanded their colonial empires by over ten million square miles and nearly one hundred fifty million people — about a fifth of the world's land area and perhaps a tenth of its population at the time — in only thirty years.

As striking as the amount of territory acquired was the deliberate and blatantly aggressive fashion in which the Europeans went about pursuing their various interests overseas. Whether a state was simply gaining formal control over areas in which it had had previous interests, such as in the Gold Coast or Madagascar; whether several states were competing for influence, such as in China, the Sudan, or Morocco; or whether states were disputing over areas previously colonized, such as in the Transvaal, they behaved in a fashion which kept them perpetually involved in diplomatic crises with each other and in exciting but usually one-sided conflicts ("sporting wars," Bismarck once called them) with peoples overseas. While small groups of competing Europeans struggled across the plains and through the swamps of Africa and Southeast Asia and sailed among the innumerable Pacific islands, inducing the inhabitants by force or persuasion to sign treaties of protection or cession with them, the heads of state in Europe argued ceaselessly and tried to establish effective control over the great areas so tenuously acquired. A crescendo of tension and violence was reached at the end of the century with the massacre of twenty thousand dervishes by Kitchener and his British troops at Obdurman, before Khartoum, in 1898; the meeting of the French and British at Fashoda on the upper Nile, later that year, which almost brought on war between them; the war between Spain and America in 1898; the outbreak in 1899 of the three-year conflict between the British and the Boers in South Africa; and the Boxer Rebellion in China in 1900. The period of the "new imperialism," as it has been called, was, especially in contrast to the preceding years of political indifference, a time of unaccustomed belligerence.

Historians have generally agreed that the late nineteenth-century European expansion was one of the great events of world history.[1] Its impact on both European and non-European peoples was immeasurable. But while historians have accepted its importance, they have been at the same time unable to agree about the origin and nature of the events of the period, the motivations of the various participants, and the place of the movement as a whole in modern European history. Study of the period has, in fact, resulted in a series of persistent and apparently irreconcilable historical disputes.

To a certain extent this has been due to the difficulty of the problem which is involved. Satisfactory explanations and evaluations of any historical event are difficult to achieve because generalization always tends to do violence to some details, and the European overseas activities constituted an event of extraordinary magnitude and complexity. Explanations of the period must

[1] It should be pointed out that to some students of the period the differences between the earlier and later years of the century are less significant than the similarities. See, for example, J. Gallagher and R. Robinson, "The Imperialism of Free Trade," *The Economic History Review*, VI (August, 1953), 1–15.

account for an almost limitless number of complicating circumstances. Consider two of the most important: The late nineteenth century was a period not just of European, but of world-wide, expansion. In those years the United States, Japan, Australia, New Zealand, and other states either took, or advocated taking, territories overseas. Are the European and non-European expansions connected? In other words, to what extent should a generalization about the European phenomenon be able to account for the expansion throughout the world? The late nineteenth century was also a period of extensive tariff enactments. The period of free trade seemed to be over, and in the 1870's and 1880's Russia, Spain, Italy, Germany, and France raised their duties on imports drastically. Protectionists often argued for expansion and vice versa. Yet the state which acquired the most new territory, Britain, remained a free-trading country, as did Belgium and the Netherlands. What connection was there, if any, between protection and expansion?

To such inherent difficulties as these must be added further complicating factors in that the late nineteenth-century expansion aroused an intense emotional and intellectual response. While many Europeans felt exhilarated by it, others, among them many of the leading liberal, socialist, and Communist thinkers, attacked it bitterly. The "new imperialism" became a live political issue as soon as it began. And out of its details has later been drawn evidence to support not only different historical interpretations but matters of political and economic theory as well. The period has become a crucial factor in the neo-Marxist explanation of the basic weaknesses of capitalism, for example, because of its apparent relation to the First World War and to certain economic policies (such as protectionism). Other theorists have considered it as one indication that political action is motivated by the urge for power. Such theorizing puts a burden on the historically minded reader, because at the same time that he looks for logical strengths and weaknesses in the theory as a whole he has to use his independent historical knowledge to fill out and test the generalizations with fact. But the various theories developed about "imperialism" have been important ones, and the modern historian has had to cope, if not with their general implications, at least with their particular application to the late nineteenth century, in his attempts to understand the period.

One result of the various interpretative disputes which have arisen is that apparently unimportant statements of detail often reflect basic differences of opinion which the historian must anticipate. Even the date cited for the beginning of the period of European expansion may imply an interpretation of the period as a whole. Writers following nationalistic interpretations tend to favor 1870, that great watershed in the history of modern European nations. Those who emphasize diplomacy often consider 1884, when the partition of Africa began in earnest, or 1878, when the Congress of Berlin took place, to be more appropriate. Lenin, the Russian Communist leader, used the year 1876, when, he argued, "the premonopolist stage of development of West European capitalism can be said to have been completed, in the main. . . ."

The frequently used word "imperialism" is another common touchstone to basic differences. The word has been applied to the period for three quarters of a century, usually more as a term of polemic than of analysis. When one finds Joseph Schumpeter, the economist, saying that "imperialism" is "the objectless disposition on the part of a state to unlimited forcible expansion," while Lenin says that it is "the monopoly stage of capitalism," and Langer, the historian, says it is "in a sense, synonymous with the appropriation by the western nations of the largest part of the rest of the world," it is apparent that a consideration of an author's definition is a prerequisite to the study of his interpretation. In many cases the mere acceptance of a particular definition of "imperialism" is tantamount to accepting a position about the nature of the entire

period, even though the events themselves may presumably be studied and interpreted without the use of the word at all.

It is the aim of this book to help illuminate the various controversies over the origins and nature of the "new imperialism" by presenting typical points of view supported with as much evidence as space permits. In general, the selections included here are concerned with Europe as a whole, rather than with specific countries, particular overseas areas, or famous individuals. Because the material is so extensive and space is short, it would be quite impossible to include specific readings on enough separate areas and individuals to avoid partiality of selection. Fortunately, the period is well-known factually and the basic issues can largely be dealt with while staying close to the problem of Europe as a whole.

The first author whose work is excerpted below, J. Holland Rose, was not directly involved in the theoretical controversies outlined above. Few historians at the turn of the century spent much time trying to analyze the period of expansion in a broad and sweeping way. They were too concerned with the specific events going on around them and, in any case, they had not at that time traveled far from the traditional historical emphasis on politics and individuals. Rose's remarks, however, do list three "prerequisites" to expansion that later authors often seem to have overlooked: that Europe was at peace, that explorations had provided necessary information, that rapid communications facilitated holding large empires together. The reader may ask whether these "prerequisites" are a necessary part of an explanation of the period. He may also ask what brought their accomplishment about.

The next three authors whose selections are presented offer economic interpretations of the European expansion in the late nineteenth century. None of them was a professional historian. All were concerned to a great extent with matters of economic theory. Their differences stem from the fact that economic interpretations may be of many varieties, for they have been written by Communists, socialists, and capitalists — and each of the economic schools includes several shades of doctrine. The Communists, for example, all claim direct intellectual descent from the works of Marx; but Marx left somewhat incomplete and ambiguous remarks on overseas expansion. In fact he died in 1883, long before our period had reached its climax. As a result, differences about the nature of capitalist "imperialism" have arisen even among the most devoutly Marxist theoreticians.

Economic evaluations of the immediate needs which drove capitalists into political activities overseas in the late nineteenth century usually follow one, or more, of three economic explanations. They may argue that the European states of the late nineteenth century were driven to acquire overseas territories to be sure of having the raw materials needed to feed their rapidly growing industrial complexes. They may maintain that the European states needed markets, because European industries were producing far more goods than could be profitably sold at home. And they may argue that there was a need to find undeveloped areas for investment in order to absorb the great amounts of capital which had accumulated in the form of profits from industrial and financial concerns. Although some economic interpretations emphasize one or another of these elements to the virtual exclusion of the others, most mention more than one since the three explanations are not necessarily incompatible.

Economic interpretations differ most bitterly over other, more basic, aspects of the problem. While all the Communists and socialists and some of the liberals apparently agree that "imperialism" represents something seriously wrong with the existing capitalist system, they disagree over just what this dislocation is: whether or not it is inevitable, how it might be corrected, what the ultimate economic goal should be. They also argue over just how the economic forces requiring or desiring overseas expansion force or induce the government to seek

it and how these forces are related to the social structure as a whole.

The logical place to start in any economic analysis of late nineteenth-century overseas expansion is J. A. Hobson's *Imperialism*, which was first published in 1902. Of the many books and articles which were being written on the subject at the time, this book became by far the most famous and influential. Hobson considered "imperialism," along with the aggressive militarism, the growing monopolies, and the new protective tariffs on the Continent, with which he associated it, to be to a great extent the result of financial weakness in the capitalist system: financial leaders desired to expand overseas because of their wish to invest more profitably their surplus capital. But while Hobson has perhaps been the person most consistently associated with developing arguments about "economic imperialism," he was no rigorous determinist. He believed in laissez faire and in free trade. Like most economic liberals, he felt that the political and economic system of his time was basically sound and with the proper adjustments could produce peace and plenty for all. Furthermore, he pointed out a number of non-economic pressures tending to induce empire-building and subtly combined these with the financial ones. Historians have found in Hobson's book the inspiration for many different views, and every historian who has come after him has had to reckon with it in his interpretation of the period. The reader will have to examine Hobson carefully, for his thesis is subjected to much praise and much criticism in the later selections in this book, perhaps not all of it based on a reasonable summary of what he actually said.

One of the most rigorous economic interpretations of European expansion, Lenin's *Imperialism, The Highest Stage of Capitalism*, contains warm praise for Hobson's argument about investments and borrows some of his analysis — even as it chides him for advocating "bourgeois social reformism and pacifism." To Lenin, "imperialism" was an inevitable and predictable catastrophe, one of the culminating crises resulting from the internal contradictions of the capitalist system and leading to its final breakdown. Lenin's argument is important because of its author and its influence on neo-Marxist theory. While it has not convinced a great many non-Communists, it should be followed closely and without any prejudgment, for in many cases the reader may find Lenin anticipates and forestalls the sometimes hastily contrived criticism to which he has been subjected.

Following Lenin's *Imperialism* is a selection from the works of Leonard Woolf, the English Fabian socialist, whose economic interpretation is less doctrinaire than Lenin's or, in some ways, Hobson's. Economic self-interest in general is Woolf's concern. The selection contains, along with special pleading, the kinds of factual material which must be dealt with by anyone critical of economic interpretations as a whole.

The first of the critics of the economic interpretation of the "new imperialism" to be represented in these readings is, curiously, a noted economist, Joseph A. Schumpeter, who explained late nineteenth-century expansion as part of a consideration of "imperialism" in general. To Schumpeter "imperialism" was an "atavism," the result of culturally inherited political and social attitudes which hung on from a previous age when they had had a justifiable existence. While the atavism which Schumpeter felt was responsible for the nineteenth-century expansion perhaps reflected to a certain degree the pro-British, anti-German pacifism which he held during World War I, when the essay on "imperialism" was written, the argument has nevertheless become probably the most influential of all the criticisms of the economic interpretation. Perhaps this is because while it patently accepts the importance of economic forces in history it not only criticizes the specific economic interpretation of nineteenth-century European expansion but provides a challenging alternative to it. Still, one who compares Schumpeter with

Hobson may find the basic attitudes of the two men not so far apart as they at first seem, and one must therefore follow carefully the connections which each one makes between economic theory and specific historical interpretation. Whether Schumpeter's explanation is or is not more satisfactory than the economic ones is a matter of considerable debate.

Murray Greene, an American scholar, takes up the debate in an essay which is highly critical of Schumpeter's point of view. In considering this economic rebuttal, one might first ask whether or not Greene's recapitulation of Schumpeter is a fair one. One may then decide whether the line of argument destroys Schumpeter's position effectively or whether it fails to deal with his basic points. Here is an economic interpreter claiming Schumpeter is not sufficiently historical. Is this a valid criticism of Greene's thesis itself?

William L. Langer, the Harvard historian, considers the problem in a well-known article first published in *Foreign Affairs* in 1935. The arguments Langer uses both in support and in criticism of Hobson and Schumpeter raise a number of questions for the reader. Is Lenin's argument that the European overseas rivalry was to satisfy prospective future, as well as immediate, needs a satisfactory answer to Langer's point that many states did not invest heavily in newly acquired territories? How effectively does the existence of a non-industrialized expansionist state, such as Russia, destroy the economic argument? How closely is Langer's historical analysis related to his political concerns of the mid-1930's, and does this affect the validity of his remarks?

A different approach to the matter of the economic interpretation is taken by the economist Eugene Staley, who summarizes a number of the points made for and against one aspect of the problem — private overseas investment — by methodically considering each country in turn. While Staley may, by his careful organization and conciseness, satisfy many readers on this subject, others may feel that even on this matter he does not answer all the questions or deal with all the facts which have been brought forth in previous selections. It is a difficult problem even when only one aspect is dealt with, as Staley himself points out. And to the consideration of the specific arguments about Schumpeter and the economic interpreters must now be added further interpretations and comments on the period as a whole.

While Schumpeter proposes his interpretation of late nineteenth-century expansion in a general and theoretical fashion, other writers are more specific. To Carlton J. H. Hayes, the Columbia University historian, the expansion was essentially a nationalistic phenomenon, and Hayes explains the undeniably economic pronouncements and activities of the period (such as one finds in Woolf) by maintaining that economic arguments were usually *ex post facto* and by implying that there can be economic self-interest in a venture without its being the primary motive. If one accepts Hayes' many facts (some of which, such as France's relatively sluggish industrial development, Lenin also uses for *his* argument) it is still necessary to consider why the nationalistic publicists felt called upon to put forth economic arguments; what sort of people they were trying to convince, and why; what made the European countries so belligerently nationalistic at the time — whether Hayes' argument, in short, simply puts the economic interpretation back one step or whether it satisfactorily makes economic matters secondary.

Hayes finds a nationalism based on wide popular support to be the crucial factor in the late nineteenth-century expansion. Nicholas Mansergh, the Cambridge historian, has a more precise explanation — and one tied, rather, to the decisions of a few political leaders. Germany had become, by its victory over France in the Franco-Prussian War, the pivot around which European diplomacy in the latter years of the century revolved. That the international position of Germany dominated the thinking of not only the German

but of the other European governments and that therefore overseas expansion was primarily an adjunct to European diplomacy is Mansergh's argument in his book, *The Coming of the First World War*. In considering this thesis one must decide whether the motive of expansion as a vehicle of European diplomacy applies as well to Britain and to France as to Germany — and how far beyond these countries it might have had significance. One must also weigh the importance of the diplomatic decisions of a few political leaders against the evidences both of great popular support, as suggested by Hayes, and of economic pressure, as mentioned by Woolf. This leads, as many of the selections do, to the general problem of assessing the relations among the different elements of late nineteenth-century society which were involved in generating and determining a country's course of action.

In an informal introduction to a volume of essays on five statesmen who espoused overseas expansion, the noted French historian, Pierre Renouvin, touches further on this problem. In summing up the general conclusions which the careers of the five statesmen bring to his mind he emphasizes the importance of individual traits of character in motivating expansion and of forces of circumstance in directing the paths it took. These suggestions may raise as many questions as they answer. One notices that Bismarck is missing from the list of statesmen. Would his inclusion have materially altered Renouvin's generalizations? To what extent was Bismarck or any other individual able to direct the course of events? How, in short, is one to unravel the problem of the final decision-making influences upon an individual or a country?

In the final selection Hannah Arendt, the political scientist, finds virtual unanimity in favor of expansion among the various social and economic elements within each European country, but she argues that these different elements approached that common attitude from widely different directions. Her selection is drawn from the controversial book, *The Origins of Totalitarianism,* which not only recognizes both economic and nationalistic pressures for expansion in the late nineteenth century but incorporates them into a larger assessment of the period as a whole. It is an all-encompassing approach: undeniably stimulating but undeniably assertive.

The reader must try to reckon with any generalizations, such as this one, which consider the period of the "new imperialism" as a whole, for the particular importance of the period in relation to the First World War, and indeed to all of contemporary history, means that broad and conflicting generalizations will continue to be made about it. Most of the writers included in this collection of readings have in fact made re-examinations and reassessments of their own conclusions. Many of them (including Hobson, Schumpeter, Hayes, and Langer) have, in other writings, made slightly different interpretations of the period than are included here.[2]

[2] See, for example, for Hobson and Schumpeter,

The reader may become somewhat confused as he examines the interpretations pitted against each other in the selections following. He will sometimes find gaps in the logic leading to the various generalizations, or facts and questions which the authors do not deal with as he thinks they should. In this situation he should first read what else the authors have written on the subject. Then he must turn to the massive literature on the subject, a literature which will not only help him evaluate those statements he finds uncertain but which may eventually lead him to the achievement of a better and more satisfying synthesis.

in E. M. Winslow, *The Pattern of Imperialism* (New York, 1948), pp. 100–103, 235–236; for Hayes, his *Contemporary Europe since 1870,* revised ed. (New York, 1958), pp. 267–270; for Langer, his *European Alliances and Alignments, 1871–1890* (New York, 1931), pp. 283–290.

[NOTE: In order to save space all but a few of the authors' footnotes have been eliminated from the original texts of the following readings. Grammar and spelling have been left unchanged.]

The Conflict of Opinion

"Analysis of the actual course of modern Imperialism has laid bare the combination of economic and political forces which fashions it. These forces are traced to their sources in the selfish interests of certain industrial, financial, and professional classes, seeking private advantages out of a policy of imperial expansion, and using this same policy to protect them in their economic, political, and social privileges against the pressure of democracy."

— J. A. Hobson

"We have seen that the economic quintessence of imperialism is monopoly capitalism. This very fact determines its place in history, for monopoly that grew up on the basis of free competition, and precisely out of free competition, is the transition from the capitalist system to a higher social-economic order."

— V. I. Lenin

". . . it follows that capitalism is by nature anti-imperialist. Hence we can not readily derive from it such imperialist tendencies as actually exist, but must evidently see them only as alien elements, carried into the world of capitalism from the outside, supported by non-capitalist factors in modern life."

— J. A. Schumpeter

"It appears to me that the main burden of Schumpeter's argument is to show that capitalism is essentially anti-imperialist. To do this he develops a very specialized definition of imperialism . . . He also sets up a very specialized definition of capitalism, which he then shows to be inconsistent with his definition of imperialism, thereby 'proving' that capitalism is anti-imperialist."

— M. Greene

"Schumpeter, who is an eminent economist, worked out a most convincing argument to prove that imperialism has nothing to do with capitalism, and that it is certainly not a development of capitalism. . . . It is now fairly clear, I think, that the neo-Marxian critics have paid far too little attention to the imponderable, psychological ingredients of imperialism."

— W. L. Langer

"Basically the new imperialism was a nationalistic phenomenon. . . . Some capitalists undoubtedly promoted imperialism, and more profited by it. But in the last analysis it was the nationalistic masses who made it possible and who most vociferously applauded it and most constantly backed it."

— C. J. H. Hayes

"The rulers of Europe thought primarily in terms of political not economic advantage and . . . the colonial policies of the Continental states were formulated in the light of the European balance of power and designed to serve European ends. When they no longer served those ends the colonial scene slips unobtrusively into the background."

— N. MANSERGH

"Is one to believe that the action of these statesmen was determined solely by the necessities they pleaded? Must one see their imperialist doctrines as solely the result of their reasoning? Certainly not. They were all, or nearly all, driven into action by their own temperaments."

— P. RENOUVIN

THREE CONDITIONS OF EXPANSION

J. HOLLAND ROSE

J. Holland Rose (1855–1942) was one of the most famous British historians in the first third of the twentieth century. Best known, perhaps, for his series of works on the French Revolution and the Napoleonic Era (including distinguished biographies of Napoleon and Pitt), he wrote as well on nationalism and on diplomatic affairs. His works were based on careful scholarship and were written with style and distinction. *The Development of the European Nations, 1870–1900*, from which the following selection is drawn, was first published in 1905. It is a detailed account of European international relations—both within Europe and in areas overseas.

I N THE opening up of new lands by European peoples the order of events is generally somewhat as follows: first come explorers, pioneers, or missionaries. These having thrown some light on the character of a land or of its people, traders follow in their wake; and in due course factories are formed and settlements arise. The ideas of the new-comers as to the rights of property and landholding differ so widely from those of the natives, that quarrels and strifes frequently ensue. Warships and soldiers then appear on the scene; and the end of the old order of things is marked by the hoisting of the Union Jack, or the French or German tricolour. In the case of the expansion of Russia as we have seen, the procedure is far otherwise. But Africa has been for the most part explored, exploited, and annexed by agencies working from the sea and proceeding in the way just outlined.

The period since the year 1870 has for the most part witnessed the operation of the last and the least romantic of these so-called civilising efforts. The great age of African exploration was then drawing to a close. In the year 1870 that devoted missionary explorer, David Livingstone, was lost to sight for many months owing to his earnest longing peacefully to solve the great problem of the waterways of Central Africa, and thus open up an easy path for the suppression of the slave-trade. But when, in 1871, Mr. H. M. Stanley, the enterprising correspondent of the *New York Herald*, at the head of a rescue expedition, met the grizzled, fever-stricken veteran near Ujiji and greeted him with the words – "Mr. Livingstone, I presume," the age of mystery and picturesqueness vanished away.

A change in the spirit and methods of exploration naturally comes about when the efforts of single individuals give place to collective enterprise, and that change was now rapidly to come over the whole field of African exploration. The day of the Mungo Parks and Livingstones was passing away, and the day of associations and companies was at hand. In 1876, Leopold II., King of the Belgians, summoned to Brussels several of the leading explorers and geographers in order to confer on the best methods of opening up Africa. The specific results of this important Conference will be considered in the next chapter; but we may here note that, under the auspices of the "Interna-

From J. Holland Rose, *The Development of the European Nations, 1870–1900* (London, 1905), pp. 508–512. By permission of Constable & Company, Ltd.

1

tional Association for the Exploration and Civilisation of Africa" then founded, much pioneer work was carried out in districts remote from the River Congo. The vast continent also yielded up its secrets to travellers working their way in from the south and the north, so that in the late seventies the white races opened up to view vast and populous districts which imaginative chartographers in other ages had diversified with the Mountains of the Moon or with signs of the Zodiac and monstrosities of the animal creation.

The last epoch-marking work carried through by an individual was accomplished by a Scottish explorer, whose achievements almost rivalled those of Livingstone. Joseph Thomson, a native of Dumfriesshire, succeeded in 1879 to the command of an exploring party which sought to open up the country around the lakes of Nyassa and Tanganyika. Four years later, on behalf of the Royal Geographical Society, he undertook to examine the country behind Mombasa which was little better known than when Vasco da Gama first touched there. In this journey Thomson discovered two snow-capped mountains, Kilimanjaro and Kenia, and made known the resources of the country as far inland as the Victoria Nyanza. Considering the small resources he had at hand, and the cruel and warlike character of the Masai people through whom he journeyed, this journey was by far the most remarkable and important in the annals of exploration during the eighties. Thomson afterwards undertook to open a way from the Benuë, the great eastern affluent of the Niger, to Lake Chad and the White Nile. Here again he succeeded beyond all expectation, while his tactful management of the natives led to political results of the highest importance, as will shortly appear.

These explorations and those of French, German, and Portuguese travellers served to bring nearly the whole of Africa within the ken of the civilised world, and revealed the fact that nearly all parts of tropical Africa had a distinct commercial value.

This discovery, we may point out, is the necessary preliminary to any great and sustained work of colonisation and annexation. Three conditions may be looked on as essential to such an effort. First, that new lands should be known to be worth the labour of exploitation or settlement; second, that the older nations should possess enough vitality to pour settlers and treasure into them; and thirdly, that mechanical appliances should be available for the overcoming of natural obstacles.

Now, a brief glance at the great eras of exploring and colonising activity will show that in all these three directions the last thirty years have presented advantages which are unique in the history of the world. A few words will suffice to make good this assertion. The wars which constantly devastated the ancient world, and the feeble resources in regard to navigation wielded by adventurous captains, such as Hanno the Carthaginian, grievously hampered all the efforts of explorers by sea, while mechanical appliances were so weak as to cripple man's efforts at penetrating the interior. The same is true of the mediæval voyagers and travellers. Only the very princes among men, Columbus, Magellan, Vasco da Gama, Cabot, Cabral, Gilbert, and Raleigh, could have done what they did with ships that were mere playthings. Science had to do her work of long and patient research before man could hopefully face the mighty forces and malignant influences of the tropics. Nor was the advance of knowledge and invention sufficient by itself to equip man for successful war against the ocean, the desert, the forest, and the swamp. The political and social development of the older countries was equally necessary. In order that thousands of settlers should be able and ready to press in where the one great leader had shown the way, Europe had to gain something like peace and stability. Only thus, when the natural surplus of the white races could devote itself to the task of peacefully subduing the earth rather than to the hideous work of mutual slaughter, could the lifeblood of Europe be poured forth in fertilising streams into the waste places of the other continents.

The latter half of the eighteenth century promised for a brief space to inaugurate such a period of expansive life. The close of the Seven Years' War seemed to be the starting point for a peaceful campaign against the unknown; but the efforts of Cook, d'Entrecasteaux, and others then had little practical result, owing to the American War of Independence, and the great cycle of the Revolutionary and Napoleonic Wars. These in their turn left Europe too exhausted to accomplish much in the way of colonial expansion until the middle of the nineteenth century. Even then, when the steamship and the locomotive were at hand to multiply man's powers, there was, as yet, no general wish, except on the part of the more fortunate English-speaking peoples, to enter into man's new heritage. The problems of Europe had to be settled before the age of expansive activity could dawn in its full radiance. As has been previously shown, Europe was in an introspective mood up to the years 1870–1878.

Our foregoing studies have shown that the years following the Russo-Turkish War of 1877–8 brought about a state of political equilibrium which made for peace and stagnation in Europe; and the natural forces of the Continent, cramped by the opposition of equal and powerful forces, took the line of least resistance—away from Europe. For Russia, the line of least resistance was in Central Asia. For all other European States

it was the sea, and the new lands beyond.

Furthermore, in that momentous decade the steamship and locomotive were constantly gaining in efficiency; electricity was entering the arena as a new and mighty force; by this time medical science had so far advanced as to screen man from many of the ills of which the tropics are profuse; and the repeating rifle multiplied the power of the white man in his conflicts with savage peoples. When all the advantages of the present generation are weighed in the balance against the meagre equipment of the earlier discoverers, the nineteenth century has scant claim for boasting over the fifteenth. In truth, its great achievements in this sphere have been practical and political. It has only fulfilled the rich promise of the age of the great navigators. Where they could but wonderingly skirt the fringes of a new world, the moderns have won their way to the heart of things and found many an Eldorado potentially richer than that which tempted the cupidity of Cortes and Pizarro.

In one respect the European statesmen of the recent past tower above their predecessors of the centuries before. In the eighteenth century the "mercantilist" craze for seizing new markets and shutting out all possible rivals brought about most of the wars that desolated Europe. In the years 1880–1890 the great Powers put forth sustained and successful efforts to avert the like calamity, and to cloak with the mantle of diplomacy the eager scrambles for the unclaimed lands of the world.

IMPERIALISM. A STUDY

J. A. HOBSON

John A. Hobson (1858–1940) was an economist and publicist of extraordinary powers and reputation. He wrote constantly—as a regular contributor to the British *Nation* for many years and as author of some three dozen books on a wide variety of economic, political, and social topics. In the course of his career he developed a theory of underconsumption which argued that the weaknesses of contemporary capitalism resulted primarily from the maldistribution of wealth—especially oversaving by the wealthy. Hobson's solution to the economic problem included the nationalization of certain industries and the retention of private enterprise in others—which left him somewhere between the socialists and the liberals of his time. His interest in "imperialism" (which reflected an important part of his general economic theory) stemmed most directly from a trip to South Africa as a correspondent for the *Manchester Guardian* just before the Boer War. Hobson was a severe critic of British policy in South Africa and especially of the war itself. In the selections from *Imperialism* (probably his most famous book), the reader will encounter Hobson's remarkable talents of analysis and exposition.

THE MEASURE OF IMPERIALISM

QUIBBLES about the modern meaning of the term Imperialism are best resolved by reference to concrete facts in the history of the last thirty years. During that period a number of European nations, Great Britain being first and foremost, have annexed or otherwise asserted political sway over vast portions of Africa and Asia, and over numerous islands in the Pacific and elsewhere. The extent to which this policy of expansion has been carried on, and in particular the enormous size and the peculiar character of the British acquisitions, are not adequately realised even by those who pay some attention to Imperial politics.

The following lists, giving the area and, where possible, the population of the new acquisitions, are designed to give definiteness to the term Imperialism. Though derived from official sources, they do not, however, profess strict accuracy. The sliding scale of political terminology along which no-man's land, or hinterland, passes into some kind of definite protectorate is often applied so as to conceal the process; "rectification" of a fluid frontier is continually taking place; paper "partitions" of spheres of influence or protection in Africa and Asia are often obscure, and in some cases the area and the population are highly speculative.

In a few instances it is possible that portions of territory put down as acquired since 1870 may have been ear-marked by a European Power at some earlier date. But care is taken to include only such territories as have come within this period under the

From J. A. Hobson, *Imperialism. A Study* (London, 1902), pp. 15–26, 30–31, 42–44, 46, 47–48, 50–68, 76–79, 85–86, 207–211, 224–234. Reprinted by permission of George Allen & Unwin Ltd.

	Date of Acquisition	Area. Square Miles	Population
EUROPE —			
Cyprus	1878	3,584	227,900
AFRICA —			
Zanzibar and Pemba	1888 ⎫	⎱ 1,000,000	⎧ 200,000
East Africa Protectorate	1895 ⎭		⎩ 2,500,000
Uganda Protectorate	1894–1896	140,000	3,800,000
Somali Coast Protectorate	1884–1885	68,000	(?)
British Central Africa Protectorate	1889	42,217	688,049
Lagos	to 1899	21,000	3,000,000
Gambia	to 1888	3,550	215,000
Ashantee	1896–1901	70,000	2,000,000
Niger Coast Protectorate	1885–1898	⎰ 400,000 to 500,000	25,000,000 to 40,000,000
Egypt	1882	400,000	9,734,405
Egyptian Soudan	1882	950,000	10,000,000
Griqualand West	1871–1880	15,197	83,373
Zululand	1879–1897	10,521	240,000
British Bechuanaland	1885	51,424	72,736
Bechuanaland Protectorate	1891	213,000	200,000
Transkei	1879–1885	2,535	153,582
Tembuland	1885	4,155	180,130
Pondoland	1894	4,040	188,000
Griqualand East	1879–1885	7,511	152,609
British South Africa Charter	1889	750,000	321,000
Transvaal	1900	119,139	870,000
Orange River Colony	1900	48,826	207,503
ASIA —			
Hong Kong (littoral)	1898	376	100,000
Wei-hai-wei	...	270	118,000
Socotra	1886	1,382	10,000
Upper Burma	1887	83,473	2,046,933
Baluchistan	1876–1889	130,000	500,000
Sikkim	1890	2,818	30,000
Rajputana (States)	⎫	⎧ 128,022	12,186,352
Burma (States)	⎬ since 1881	⎨ 62,661	785,800
Jammu and Kashmir	⎭	⎩ 80,000	2,543,952
Malay Protected States	1883–1895	24,849	620,000
North Borneo Company	1881	31,106	175,000
North Borneo Protectorate	1888	...	...
Sarawak	1888	50,000	500,000
British New Guinea	1888	90,540	350,000
Fiji Islands	1874	7,740	122,676

definite political control of the Power to which they are assigned. The figures in the case of Great Britain are so startling as to call for a little further interpretation. I have thought it right to add to the recognised list of colonies and protectorates the "veiled Protectorate" of Egypt, with its vast Soudanese claim, the entire territories assigned to Chartered Companies, and the native or feudatory States in India which acknowledge our paramountcy by the admission of a British Agent or other official endowed with real political control.

All these lands are rightly accredited to the British Empire, and if our past policy is still pursued, the intensive as distinct from the extensive Imperialism will draw them under an ever-tightening grasp.

In a few other instances, as, for example, in West Africa, countries are included in this list where some small dominion had obtained before 1870, but where the vast majority of the present area of the colony is of recent acquisition. Any older colonial possession thus included in Lagos or Gambia is, however, far more than counterbalanced by the increased area of the Gold Coast Colony, which is not included in this list, and which grew from 29,000 square miles in 1873 to 39,000 square miles in 1893.

The list is by no means complete. It takes no account of several large regions which have passed under the control of our Indian Government as native or feudatory States, but of which no statistics of area or population, even approximate, are available. Such are the Shan States, the Burma Frontier, and the Upper Burma Frontier, the districts of Chitral, Bajam, Swat, Waziristan, which came under our "sphere of influence" in 1893, and have been since taken under a closer protectorate. The increase of British India itself between 1871 and 1891 amounted to an area of 104,993 square miles, with a population of 25,-330,000, while no reliable measurement of the formation of new native States within that period and since is available. Many of the measurements here given are in round numbers, indicative of their uncertainty, but they are taken, wherever available, from official publications of the Colonial Office, corroborated or supplemented from the "Statesman's Year-book." They will by no means comprise the full tale of our expansion during the thirty years, for many enlargements made by the several colonies themselves are omitted. But taken as they stand they make a for-

midable addition to the growth of an Empire whose nucleus is only 120,000 square miles, with 40,000,000 population.

For so small a nation to add to its domains in the course of a single generation an area of 4,754,000 square miles, with an estimated population of 88,000,000, is a historical fact of great significance.

Accepting Sir Robert Giffen's estimate[1] of the size of our Empire (including Egypt and the Soudan) at about 13,000,000 square miles, with a population of some 400 to 420 millions (of whom about 50,000,000 are of British race and speech), we find that one-third of this Empire, containing quite one-fourth of the total population of the Empire, has been acquired within the last generation. This is in tolerably close agreement with other independent estimates.

The character of this Imperial expansion is clearly exhibited in the list of new territories.

Though, for convenience, the year 1870 has been taken as indicative of the beginning of a conscious policy of Imperialism, it will be evident that the movement did not attain its full impetus until the middle of the eighties. The vast increase of territory, and the method of wholesale partition which assigned to us great tracts of African land, may be dated from about 1884. Within fifteen years some three and three-quarter millions of square miles have been added to the British Empire.

Nor does Great Britain stand alone in this enterprise. The leading characteristic of modern Imperialism, the competition of rival Empires, is the product of this same period. The close of the Franco-German war marks the beginning of a new colonial policy in France and Germany, destined to take effect in the next decade. It was not unnatural that the newly-founded German Empire, surrounded by powerful enemies and doubtful allies, and perceiving its more adventurous youth drawn into the United

[1] Sir Robert Giffen: chief of the statistical department of the Board of Trade in the late nineteenth century. [Editor's note]

States and other foreign lands, should form the idea of a colonial empire. During the seventies a vigorous literature sprang up in advocacy of the policy which took shape a little later in the powerful hands of Bismarck. The earliest instance of official aid for the promotion of German commerce abroad occurred in 1880 in the Government aid granted to the "German Commercial and Plantation Association of the Southern Seas." German connection with Samoa dates from the same year, but the definite advance of Germany upon its Imperialist career began in 1884, with a policy of African protectorates and annexations of Oceanic islands. During the next fifteen years she brought under her colonial sway about 1,000,000 square miles, with an estimated population of 14,000,000. Almost the whole of this territory is tropical, and the white population forms a total of a few thousands.

Similarly in France a great revival of the old colonial spirit took place in the early eighties, the most influential of the revivalists being the eminent economist, M. Paul Leroy-Beaulieu. The extension of empire in Senegal and Sahara in 1880 was followed next year by the annexation of Tunis, and France was soon actively engaged in the scramble for Africa in 1884, while at the same time she was fastening her rule on Tonking and Laos in Asia. Her acquisitions since 1880 (exclusive of the extension of New Caledonia and its dependencies) amount to an area of over three and a half million square miles, with a native population of some 37,000,000, almost the whole tropical or sub-tropical, inhabited by lower races and incapable of genuine French colonisation.

Italian aspirations took similar shape from 1880 onwards, though the disastrous experience of the Abyssinian expeditions has given a check to Italian Imperialism.[2] Her possessions in East Africa are con-fined to the northern colony of Eritrea and the protectorate of Somaliland.

Of the other European States, two only, Portugal and Belgium, enter directly into the competition of the new Imperialism. The African arrangements of 1884–6 assigned to Portugal the large district of Angola on the Congo Coast, while a large strip of East Africa passed definitely under her political control in 1891. The anomalous position of the great Congo Free State, ceded to the King of Belgium in 1883, and growing since then by vast accretions, must be regarded as involving Belgium in the competition for African empire.

Spain may be said to have definitely retired from imperial competition. The large and important possessions of Holland in the East and West Indies, though involving her in imperial politics to some degree, belong to older colonialism: she takes no part in the new imperial expansion.

Russia, the only active expansionist country of the North, stands alone in the character of her imperial growth, which differs from other Imperialism in that it has been principally Asiatic in its achievements and has proceeded by direct extension of imperial boundaries, partaking to a larger extent than in the other cases of a regular colonial policy of settlement for purposes of agriculture and industry. It is, however, evident that Russian expansion, though of a more normal and natural order than that which characterises the new Imperialism, comes definitely into contact and into competition with the claims and aspirations of the latter in Asia, and has been advancing rapidly during the period which is the object of our study.

The recent entrance of the powerful and progressive nation of the United States of America upon Imperialism by the annexation of Hawaii and the taking over of the relics of ancient Spanish empire not only adds a new formidable competitor for trade

[2] In 1887–89 and 1895–96, the Italians undertook two major expeditions into Ethiopia, both militarily undistinguished. At Adowa (or Adua) in 1896, the advancing Italian forces were virtually destroyed in one of the most crushing European defeats by a non-European army in modern times. [Editor's note]

and territory, but changes and complicates the issues. As the focus of political attention and activity shifts more to the Pacific States, and the commercial aspirations of America are more and more set upon trade with the Pacific islands and the Asiatic coast, the same forces which are driving European States along the path of territorial expansion seem likely to act upon the United States, leading her to a virtual abandonment of the principle of American isolation which has hitherto dominated her policy.

The following comparative table of colonisation, compiled from the "Statesman's Year-book" for 1900 by Mr. H. C. Morris, marks the present expansion of the political control of Western nations: —

	Number of Colonies	Area. Square Miles		Population	
		Mother Country	Colonies, &c.	Mother Country	Colonies, &c.
United Kingdom	50	120,979	11,605,238	40,559,954	345,222,239
France	33	204,092	3,740,756	38,517,975	56,401,860
Germany	13	208,830	1,027,120	52,279,901	14,687,000
Netherlands	3	12,648	782,862	5,074,632	35,115,711
Portugal	9	36,038	801,100	5,049,729	9,148,707
Spain	3	197,670	243,877	17,565,632	136,000
Italy	2	110,646	188,500	31,856,675	850,000
Austria-Hungary	2	241,032	23,570	41,244,811	1,568,092
Denmark	3	15,289	86,634	2,185,335	114,229
Russia	3	8,660,395	255,550	128,932,173	15,684,000
Turkey	4	1,111,741	465,000	23,834,500	14,956,236
China	5	1,336,841	2,881,560	386,000,000	16,680,000
U. S. A.	6	3,557,000	172,091	77,000,000	10,544,617
Total	136	15,813,201	22,273,858	850,103,317	521,108,791

The political nature of the new British Imperialism may be authoritatively ascertained by considering the governmental relations which the newly annexed territories hold with the Crown.

Officially, British "colonial possessions" fall into three classes — (1) "Crown colonies, in which the Crown has the entire control of legislation, while the administration is carried on by public officers under the control of the Home Government; (2) colonies possessing representative institutions, but not responsible government, in which the Crown has no more than a veto on legislation, but the Home Government retains the control of public affairs; (3) colonies possessing representative institutions and responsible government, in which the Crown has only a veto on legislation, and the Home Government has no control over any officer except the Governor."

Now, of the thirty-nine separate areas which have been annexed by Great Britain since 1870 as colonies or protectorates, not a single one ranks in class 2 or 3. The new Imperialism has established no single British colony endowed with responsible government or representative institutions. Nor, with the exception of the three new States in South Africa, where white settlers live in some numbers, is it seriously pretended that any of these annexed territories is being prepared and educated for representative, responsible self-government; and even in these South African States there is no serious intention, either on the part of the Home Government or of the colonists, that the majority of the inhabitants shall have any real voice in the government.

It is true that some of these areas enjoy

a measure of self-government, as protectorates or as feudatory States, under their own native princes. But all these in major matters of policy are subject to the absolute rule of the British Government, or of some British official, while the general tendency is towards drawing the reins of arbitrary control more tightly over protectorates, converting them into States which are in substance, though not always in name, Crown colonies. With the exception of a couple of experiments in India, the tendency everywhere has been towards a closer and more drastic imperial control over the territories that have been annexed, transforming protectorates, company rule, and spheres of influence into definite British States of the Crown colony order.

This is attributable, not to any greed of tyranny on the part of the Imperial Government, but to the conditions imposed upon our rule by considerations of climate and native population. Almost the whole of this new territory is tropical, or so near to the tropics as to preclude genuine colonisation of British settlers, while in those few districts where Europeans can work and breed, as in parts of South Africa and Egypt, the preoccupation of the country by large native populations of "lower races" precludes any considerable settlement of British workers and the safe bestowal of the full self-government which prevails in Australasia and Canada.

The same is true to an even more complete extent of the Imperialism of other continental countries. The new Imperialism has nowhere extended the political and civil liberties of the mother country to any part of the vast territories which, since 1870, have fallen under the government of Western civilised Powers. Politically, the new Imperialism is an expansion of autocracy.

Taking the growth of Imperialism as illustrated in the recent expansion of Great Britain and of the chief continental Powers, we find the distinction between Imperialism and colonisation, set forth in the opening chapter, closely borne out by facts and figures, and warranting the following general judgments:

First — Almost the whole of recent imperial expansion is occupied with the political absorption of tropical or sub-tropical lands in which white men will not settle with their families.

Second — Nearly all the lands are thickly peopled by "lower races."

Thus this recent imperial expansion stands entirely distinct from the colonisation of sparsely peopled lands in temperate zones, where white colonists carry with them the modes of government, the industrial and other arts of the civilisation of the mother country. The "occupation" of these new territories is comprised in the presence of a small minority of white men, officials, traders, and industrial organisers, exercising political and economic sway over great hordes of population regarded as inferior and as incapable of exercising any considerable rights of self-government, in politics or industry.

THE COMMERCIAL VALUE OF IMPERIALISM

The absorption of so large a proportion of public interest, energy, blood and money in seeking to procure colonial possessions and foreign markets would seem to indicate that Great Britain obtains her chief livelihood by external trade. Now this is not the case. Large as is our foreign and colonial trade in volume and in value, essential as is much of it to our national well-being, nevertheless it furnishes a small proportion of the real income of the nation.

Although the volume and value of home industries are not directly calculable, the total income of the nation, comprising profits, wages, rents, and other gains from all sources, is approximately estimated at £1,700,000,000 per annum. This sum, of course, covers all payments, not only for productive services of land, capital and labour in the making and distributing of material wealth, but for professional and personal services as well. Real income in the shape of goods or services to this amount is consumed or saved within the year.

Now the total value of the import and export trade of Great Britain in 1898 (we take this year as the latest normal one for the purpose, later years being disturbed by the war factor) amounted to £765,000,000. If we were to take the very liberal allowance of 5 per cent as profit upon this turnover of trade, the annual income directly derived from our external trade would amount to a little over £38,000,000, or about one forty-fifth part of our total income.

* * *

. . . Taking under survey our whole Empire, we reach the conclusion that, excluding our commerce with India, the smallest, least valuable, and most uncertain trade is that done with our tropical possessions, and in particular with those which have come under imperial control since 1870. The only considerable increase of our import trade since 1884 is from our genuine colonies in Australasia, North America, and Cape Colony; the trade with India has been stagnant, while that with our tropical colonies in Africa and the West Indies has been in most cases irregular and dwindling. Our export trade exhibits the same general character, save that Australia and Canada show a growing resolution to release themselves from dependence upon British manufactures; the trade with the tropical colonies, though exhibiting some increase, is very small and very fluctuating.

As for the territories acquired under the new Imperialism, except in one instance, no serious attempt to regard them as satisfactory business assets is possible. Egypt alone yields a trade of some magnitude; of the other possessions, three only – Lagos, Niger Coast Protectorate, and North Borneo – are proved to do a trade with Great Britain exceeding one million pounds in value. In fact, excluding Egypt, the whole volume of this trade, so far as it is officially recorded, does not amount to ten million pounds; and though the actual trade is doubtless in excess of this sum, it forms an infinitesimal addition to the commercial resources of our nation. Apart from its quantity, the quality of the new tropical export trade is of the lowest, consisting for the most part, as the analysis of the Colonial Office shows, of the cheapest metal goods of Birmingham and Sheffield, and large quantities of gunpowder, spirits, and tobacco.

Such evidence leads to the following conclusions bearing upon the economics of the new Imperialism. First, the external trade of Great Britain bears a small and diminishing proportion to its internal industry and trade. Secondly, of the external trade, that with British possessions bears a diminishing proportion to that with foreign countries. Thirdly, of the trade with British possessions, the tropical trade, and in particular the trade with the new tropical possessions, is the smallest, least progressive, and most fluctuating in quantity, while it is lowest in the character of the goods which it embraces.

IMPERIALISM AS AN OUTLET FOR POPULATION

There is a widely prevalent belief that imperial expansion is desirable, or even necessary, in order to absorb and utilise the surplus of our ever-growing population. . . .
. . . What validity does it possess as an argument for recent imperial expansion?

Let me first ask: Is England over-populated now, and is the prospect of further increase such as to compel us to "peg out claims for posterity" in other parts of the world? The facts are these. Great Britain is not so thickly populated as certain prosperous industrial areas in Germany, the Netherlands, and China: along with every recent growth of population has come a far greater growth of wealth and of the power to purchase food and other subsistence. The modern specialisation of industry has caused a congestion of population upon certain spots which may be injurious in some ways to the well-being of the nation, but it cannot be regarded as over-population in the sense of a people outgrowing the means of subsistence. Nor have we reason to fear such over-population in the future. It is true that our manufactures and commerce may not continue to grow as rapidly as in the past, though we have no clear warrant from industrial statistics for this judgment: but if this be so, neither is our population likely to increase so fast. Of this we have clear statistical evidence: the diminution of the rate of growth of our population, as disclosed by the two latest censuses, is such as to justify the conclusion that, if the same forces continue to operate, the population of Great Britain will be stationary by the middle of the century.

There exists, then, no general necessity for a policy of expansion in order to provide for over-population, present or prospective. But supposing it were necessary for an increasing surplus of our population to emigrate, is it necessary for us to spend so large a part of our national resources, and to incur such heavy risks, in seizing new territory for them to settle upon? . . .

No substantial settlement of Britons is taking place upon any of the areas of the Empire acquired since 1870, excepting the Transvaal and the Orange River Colony, nor is it likely that any such settlement will take place. The tropical character of most lands acquired under the new Imperialism renders genuine colonisation impossible: there is no true British settlement in these places; a small number of men spend a short broken period in precarious occupations as traders, engineers, missionaries, overseers. The new Empire is even more barren for settlement than for profitable trade.

Economic Parasites of Imperialism

I

Seeing that the Imperialism of the last three decades is clearly condemned as a business policy, in that at enormous expense it has procured a small, bad, unsafe increase of markets, and has jeopardised the entire wealth of the nation in rousing the strong resentment of other nations, we may ask, "How is the British nation induced to embark upon such unsound business?" The only possible answer is that the business interests of the nation as a whole are subordinated to those of certain sectional interests that usurp control of the national resources and use them for their private gain. This is no strange or monstrous charge to bring; it is the commonest disease of all forms of government. The famous words of Sir Thomas More are as true now as when he wrote them: "Everywhere do I perceive a certain conspiracy of rich men seeking their own advantage under the name and pretext of the commonwealth."

Although the new Imperialism has been bad business for the nation, it has been good business for certain classes and certain trades within the nation. The vast expenditure on armaments, the costly wars, the grave risks and embarrassments of foreign policy, the stoppage of political and social reforms within Great Britain, though fraught with great injury to the nation, have served well the present business interests of certain industries and professions.

It is idle to meddle with politics unless we clearly recognise this central fact and understand what these sectional interests are which are the enemies of national safety and the commonwealth. We must put aside the merely sentimental diagnosis which explains wars or other national blunders by outbursts of patriotic animosity or errors of statecraft. Doubtless at every outbreak of war not only the man in the street but the man at the helm is often duped by the cunning with which aggressive motives and greedy purposes dress themselves in defensive clothing. There is, it may be safely asserted, no war within memory, however nakedly aggressive it may seem to the dispassionate historian, which has not been presented to the people who were called upon to fight as a necessary defensive policy, in which the honour, perhaps the very existence, of the State was involved.

The disastrous folly of these wars, the material and moral damage inflicted even on the victor, appear so plain to the disinterested spectator that he is apt to despair of any State attaining years of discretion, and inclines to regard these natural cataclysms as implying some ultimate irrationalism in politics. But careful analysis of the existing relations between business and politics shows that the aggressive Imperialism which we seek to understand is not in the main the product of blind passions of races or of the mixed folly and ambition of politicians. It is far more rational than at first sight appears. Irrational from the standpoint of the whole nation, it is rational enough from the standpoint of certain classes in the nation. A completely socialist State which kept good books and presented regular balance-sheets of expenditure and assets would soon discard Imperialism; an intelligent *laissez-faire* democracy which gave duly proportionate weight in its policy to all economic interests alike would do the same. But a State in which certain well-organised business interests are able to outweigh the weak, diffused interest of the community is bound to pursue a policy which accords with the pressure of the former interests.

In order to explain Imperialism on this hypothesis we have to answer two questions. Do we find in Great Britain to-day any well-organised group of special commercial and social interests which stand to gain by aggressive Imperialism and the militarism it involves? If such a combination of interests exists, has it the power to work its will in the arena of politics?

What is the direct economic outcome of Imperialism? A great expenditure of public money upon ships, guns, military and naval equipment and stores, growing and productive of enormous profits when a war, or an alarm of war, occurs; new public loans and important fluctuations in the home and foreign Bourses; more posts for soldiers and sailors and in the diplomatic and consular services; improvement of foreign investments by the substitution of the British flag for a foreign flag; acquisition of markets for certain classes of exports, and some protection and assistance for trades representing British houses in these manufactures; employment for engineers, missionaries, speculative miners, ranchers and other emigrants.

Certain definite business and professional interests feeding upon imperialistic expenditure, or upon the results of that expenditure, are thus set up in opposition to the common good, and, instinctively feeling their way to one another, are found united in strong sympathy to support every new imperialist exploit.

If the £60,000,000 which may now be taken as a minimum expenditure on armaments in time of peace were subjected to a close analysis, most of it would be traced directly to the tills of certain big firms engaged in building warships and transports, equipping and coaling them, manufacturing guns, rifles, and ammunition, supplying horses, waggons, saddlery, food, clothing for the services, contracting for barracks, and for other large irregular needs. Through these main channels the millions flow to feed many subsidiary trades, most of which are quite aware that they are engaged in executing contracts for the services. Here we have an important nucleus of commercial Imperialism. Some of these trades, especially the shipbuilding, boiler-making, and gun and ammunition making trades, are conducted by large firms with immense capital, whose heads are well aware of the uses of political influence for trade purposes.

These men are Imperialists by conviction; a pushful policy is good for them.

With them stand the great manufacturers for export trade, who gain a living by supplying the real or artificial wants of the new countries we annex or open up. Manchester, Sheffield, Birmingham, to name three representative cases, are full of firms which compete in pushing textiles and hardware, engines, tools, machinery, spirits, guns, upon new markets. The public debts which ripen in our colonies, and in foreign countries that come under our protectorate or influence, are largely loaned in the shape of rails, engines, guns, and other materials of civilisation made and sent out by British firms. The making of railways, canals, and other public works, the establishment of factories, the development of mines, the improvement of agriculture in new countries, stimulate a definite interest in important manufacturing industries which feeds a very firm imperialist faith in their owners.

The proportion which such trade bears to the total industry of Great Britain is very small, but some of it is extremely influential and able to make a definite impression upon politics, through chambers of commerce, Parliamentary representatives, and semi-political, semi-commercial bodies like the Imperial South African Association or the China League.

The shipping trade has a very definite interest which makes for Imperialism. This is well illustrated by the policy of State subsidies now claimed by shipping firms as a retainer, and in order to encourage British shipping for purposes of imperial safety and defence.

The services are, of course, imperialist by conviction and by professional interest, and every increase of the army and navy enhances their numerical strength and the political power they exert. The abolition of purchase in the army, by opening the profession to the upper middle classes, greatly enlarged this most direct feeder of imperial

sentiment. The potency of this factor is, of course, largely due to the itch for glory and adventure among military officers upon disturbed or uncertain frontiers of the Empire. This has been a most prolific source of expansion in India. The direct professional influence of the services carries with it a less organised but powerful sympathetic support on the part of the aristocracy and the wealthy classes, who seek in the services careers for their sons.

To the military services we may add the Indian Civil Service and the numerous official and semi-official posts in our colonies and protectorates. Every expansion of the Empire is also regarded by these same classes as affording new openings for their sons as ranchers, planters, engineers, or missionaries. This point of view is aptly summarised by a high Indian official, Sir Charles Crossthwaite, in discussing British relations with Siam. "The real question was who was to get the trade with them, and how we could make the most of them, so as to find fresh markets for our goods and also employment for those superfluous articles of the present day, our boys."

From this standpoint our colonies still remain what James Mill cynically described them as being, "a vast system of outdoor relief for the upper classes."

In all the professions, military and civil, the army, diplomacy, the church, the bar, teaching and engineering, Greater Britain serves for an overflow, relieving the congestion of the home market and offering chances to more reckless or adventurous members, while it furnishes a convenient limbo for damaged characters and careers. The actual amount of profitable employment thus furnished by our recent acquisitions is inconsiderable, but it arouses that disproportionate interest which always attaches to the margin of employment. To extend this margin is a powerful motive in Imperialism.

These influences, primarily economic, though not unmixed with other sentimental motives, are particularly operative in military, clerical, academic, and Civil Service circles, and furnish an interested bias towards Imperialism throughout the educated classes.

II

By far the most important economic factor in Imperialism is the influence relating to investments. The growing cosmopolitanism of capital is the greatest economic change of this generation. Every advanced industrial nation is tending to place a larger share of its capital outside the limits of its own political area, in foreign countries, or in colonies, and to draw a growing income from this source.

No exact or even approximate estimate of the total amount of the income of the British nation derived from foreign investments is possible. We possess, however, in the income-tax assessments an indirect measurement of certain large sections of investments, from which we can form some judgment as to the total size of the income from foreign and colonial sources, and the rate of its growth.

INCOME FROM FOREIGN INVESTMENTS ASSURED TO INCOME-TAX

	1884	1888	1892	1896	1900
	£	£	£	£	£
From Indian public revenue	2,607,942	3,130,959	3,203,573	3,475,751	3,587,919
Indian rails	4,544,466	4,841,647	4,580,797	4,543,969	4,693,795
Colonial and foreign public securities, &c.	13,233,271	16,757,736	14,949,017	16,419,933	18,394,380
Railways out of United Kingdom	3,777,592	4,178,456	8,013,838	13,032,556	14,043,107
Foreign and colonial investments	9,665,853	18,069,573	23,981,545	17,428,870	19,547,685
	33,829,124	46,978,371	54,728,770	54,901,079	60,266,886

From this table it appears that the period of energetic Imperialism has been coincident with a remarkable growth in the income from external investments. The income from these sources has nearly doubled in the period 1884–1900, while the portion derived from foreign railways and foreign and colonial investments has increased at a still more rapid rate.

These figures only give the foreign income which can be identified as such. To them must be added a large amount of income which escapes these income-tax returns, including considerable sums which would appear as profits of businesses carried on in the United Kingdom, such as insurance companies, investment trusts, and land mortgage companies, many of which derive a large part of their income from foreign investments. How rapid is the growth of this order of investment is seen from the published returns of investments of life insurance companies, which show that their investments in mortgages outside the United Kingdom had grown from about £6,000,000 in 1890 to £13,000,000 in 1898.

Sir R. Giffen estimated the income derived from foreign sources as profit, interest and pensions in 1882 at £70,000,000, and in a paper read before the Statistical Society in March 1899 he estimated the income from these same sources for the current year at £90,000,000. It is probable that this last figure is an underestimate, for if the items of foreign income not included as such under the income-tax returns bear the same proportion to those included as in 1882, the present total of income from foreign and colonial investments should be £120,000,000 rather than £90,000,000. Sir R. Giffen hazards the calculation that the new public investments abroad in the sixteen years 1882–1898 amounted to over £800,000,000, "and though part of the sum may have been nominal only, the real investment must have been enormous."

Mr. Mulhall[3] gives the following estimate of the size and growth of our foreign and colonial investments since 1862:

Year	Amount	Annual Increase
	£	Per Cent
1862	144,000,000	...
1872	600,000,000	45.6
1882	875,000,000	27.5
1893	1,698,000,000	74.8

This last amount is of especial interest, because it represents the most thorough investigation made by a most competent economist for the "Dictionary of Political Economy." The investments included under this figure may be classified under the following general heads:

Loans	Million £
Foreign	525
Colonial	225
Municipal	20
	770

Railways	Million £
U.S.A.	120
Colonial	140
Various	128
	388

Sundries	Million £
Banks	50
Lands	100
Mines, &c.	390
	540

[3] Michael G. Mulhall: British editor and statistician. [Editor's note]

In other words, in 1893 the British capital invested abroad represented about 15 per cent of the total wealth of the United Kingdom: nearly one-half of this capital was in the form of loans to foreign and colonial Governments; of the rest a large proportion was invested in railways, banks, telegraphs, and other public services, owned, controlled, or vitally affected by Governments, while most of the remainder was placed in lands and mines, or in industries directly dependent on land values.

Income-tax returns and other statistics descriptive of the growth of these investments indicate that the total amount of British investments abroad at the end of the nineteenth century cannot be set down at a lower figure than £2,000,000,000. Considering that Sir R. Giffen regarded as "moderate" the estimate of £1,700,000,000 in 1892, the figure here named is probably below the truth.

Now, without placing any undue reliance upon these estimates, we cannot fail to recognise that in dealing with these foreign investments we are facing by far the most important factor in the economics of Imperialism. Whatever figures we take, two facts are evident. First, that the income derived as interest upon foreign investments enormously exceeds that derived as profits upon ordinary export and import trade. Secondly, that while our foreign and colonial trade, and presumably the income from it, are growing but slowly, the share of our import values representing income from foreign investments is growing very rapidly.

In a former chapter I pointed out how small a proportion of our national income appeared to be derived as profits from external trade. It seemed unintelligible that the enormous costs and risks of the new Imperialism should be undertaken for such small results in the shape of increase to external trade, especially when the size and character of the new markets acquired were taken into consideration. The statistics of foreign investments, however, shed clear light upon the economic forces which are dominating our policy. While the manu-facturing and trading classes make little out of their new markets, paying, if they knew it, much more in taxation than they get out of them in trade, it is quite other-wise with the investor.

It is not too much to say that the modern foreign policy of Great Britain is primarily a struggle for profitable markets of invest-ment. To a larger extent every year Great Britain is becoming a nation living upon tribute from abroad, and the classes who enjoy this tribute have an ever-increasing incentive to employ the public policy, the public purse, and the public force to extend the field of their private investments, and to safeguard and improve their existing investments. This is, perhaps, the most important fact in modern politics, and the obscurity in which it is wrapped constitutes the gravest danger to our State.

What is true of Great Britain is true likewise of France, Germany, the United States, and of all countries in which mod-ern capitalism has placed large surplus savings in the hands of a plutocracy or of a thrifty middle class. A well-recognised distinction is drawn between creditor and debtor countries. Great Britain has been for some time by far the largest creditor country, and the policy by which the in-vesting classes use the instrument of the State for private business purposes is most richly illustrated in the recent history of her wars and annexations. But France, Germany, and the United States are ad-vancing fast along the same path. The nature of these imperialist operations is thus set forth by the Italian economist Loria:

When a country which has contracted a debt is unable, on account of the slenderness of its income, to offer sufficient guarantee for the punctual payment of interest, what hap-pens? Sometimes an out-and-out conquest of the debtor country follows. Thus France's attempted conquest of Mexico during the sec-ond empire was undertaken solely with the view of guaranteeing the interest of French citizens holding Mexican securities. But more frequently the insufficient guarantee of an international loan gives rise to the appoint-ment of a financial commission by the creditor countries in order to protect their rights and guard the fate of their invested capital. The appointment of such a commission literally amounts in the end, however, to a veritable conquest. We have examples of this in Egypt, which has to all practical purposes become a British province, and in Tunis, which has in like manner become a dependency of France, who supplied the greater part of the loan. The Egyptian revolt against the foreign domination issuing from the debt came to nothing, as it met with invariable opposition from capital-istic combinations, and Tel-el-Kebir's[4] success, bought with money, was the most brilliant victory wealth has ever obtained on the field of battle.

But, though useful to explain certain economic facts, the terms "creditor" and "debtor," as applied to countries, obscure the most significant feature of this Imperi-alism. For though, as appears from the analysis given above, much, if not most, of the debts are "public," the credit is nearly always private, though sometimes, as in the case of Egypt, its owners succeed in getting their Government to enter a most unprofit-able partnership, guaranteeing the payment of the interest, but not sharing in it.

Aggressive Imperialism, which costs the tax-payer so dear, which is of so little value to the manufacturer and trader, which is fraught with such grave incalculable peril to the citizen, is a source of great gain to the investor who cannot find at home the profitable use he seeks for his capital, and insists that his Government should help him to profitable and secure investments abroad.

If, contemplating the enormous expendi-ture on armaments, the ruinous wars, the diplomatic audacity of knavery by which modern Governments seek to extend their territorial power, we put the plain, practical question, *Cui bono?* the first and most ob-vious answer is, The investor.

4 Site of British victory over Egyptians, 1882. [Editor's note]

The annual income Great Britain derives from commissions on her whole foreign and colonial trade, import and export, is estimated by Sir R. Giffen at £18,000,000 for 1899, taken at 2½ per cent, upon a turnover of £800,000,000. This is the whole that we are entitled to regard as profits on external trade. Considerable as this sum is, it cannot serve to yield an economic motive-power adequate to explain the dominance which business considerations exercise over our imperial policy. Only when we set beside it some £90,000,000 or £100,000,000, representing pure profit upon investments, do we understand whence the economic impulse to Imperialism is derived.

Investors who have put their money in foreign lands, upon terms which take full account of risks connected with the political conditions of the country, desire to use the resources of their Government to minimise these risks, and so to enhance the capital value and the interest of their private investments. The investing and speculative classes in general also desire that Great Britain should take other foreign areas under her flag in order to secure new areas for profitable investment and speculation.

III

If the special interest of the investor is liable to clash with the public interest and to induce a wrecking policy, still more dangerous is the special interest of the financier, the general dealer in investments. In large measure the rank and file of the investors are, both for business and for politics, the cat's-paws of the great financial houses, who use stocks and shares not so much as investments to yield them interest, but as material for speculation in the money market. In handling large masses of stocks and shares, in floating companies, in manipulating fluctuations of values, the magnates of the Bourse find their gain. These great businesses — banking, broking, bill discounting, loan floating, company promoting — form the central ganglion of international capitalism. United by the strongest bonds of organisation, always in closest and quickest touch with one another, situated in the very heart of the business capital of every State, controlled, so far as Europe is concerned, chiefly by men of a single and peculiar race, who have behind them many centuries of financial experience, they are in a unique position to control the policy of nations. No great quick direction of capital is possible save by their consent and through their agency. Does any one seriously suppose that a great war could be undertaken by any European State, or a great State loan subscribed, if the house of Rothschild and its connections set their face against it?

Every great political act involving a new flow of capital, or a large fluctuation in the values of existing investments, must receive the sanction and the practical aid of this little group of financial kings. These men, holding their realised wealth and their business capital, as they must, chiefly in stocks and bonds, have a double stake, first as investors, but secondly and chiefly as financial dealers. As investors, their political influence does not differ essentially from that of the smaller investors, except that they usually possess a practical control of the businesses in which they invest. As speculators or financial dealers they constitute, however, the gravest single factor in the economics of Imperialism.

To create new public debts, to float new companies, and to cause constant considerable fluctuations of values are three conditions of their profitable business. Each condition carries them into politics, and throws them on the side of Imperialism.

The public financial arrangements for the Philippine war put several millions of dollars into the pockets of Mr. Pierpont Morgan and his friends; the China-Japan war, which saddled the Celestial Empire for the first time with a public debt, and the indemnity which she will pay to her European invaders in connection with the recent conflict, bring grist to the financial mills in Europe; every railway or mining concession wrung from some reluctant foreign potentate means profitable business in raising capital and floating companies. A policy which rouses fears of aggression in Asiatic states, and which fans the rivalry of commercial nations in Europe, evokes vast expenditure on armaments, and ever-accumulating public debts, while the doubts and risks accruing from this policy promote that constant oscillation of values of securities which is so profitable to the skilled financier. There is not a war, a revolution, an anarchist assassination, or any other public shock, which is not gainful to these men; they are harpies who suck their gains from every new forced expenditure and every sudden disturbance of public credit. To the financiers "in the know" the Jameson raid[5] was a most advantageous coup, as may be ascertained by a comparison of the "holdings" of these men before and after that event; the terrible sufferings of England and South Africa in the war, which is a sequel of the raid, is a source of immense profit to the big financiers who have best held out against the uncalculated waste, and have recouped themselves by profitable war contracts and by "freezing out" the smaller interests in the Transvaal. These men are the only certain gainers from the war, and most of their gains are made out of the public losses of their adopted country or the private losses of their fellow-countrymen.

The policy of these men, it is true, does not necessarily make for war; where war would bring about too great and too permanent a damage to the substantial fabric of industry, which is the ultimate and essential basis of speculation, their influence is cast for peace, as in the dangerous quarrel between Great Britain and the United States regarding Venezuela. But every increase of public expenditure, every oscillation of public credit short of this collapse, every risky enterprise in which public resources can be made the pledge of private speculations, is profitable to the big money-lender and speculator.

The wealth of these houses, the scale of their operations, and their cosmopolitan organisation make them the prime determinants of imperial policy. They have the largest definite stake in the business of Imperialism, and the amplest means of forcing their will upon the policy of nations.

In view of the part which the non-economic factors of patriotism, adventure, military enterprise, political ambition, and philanthropy play in imperial expansion, it may appear that to impute to financiers so much power is to take a too narrowly economic view of history. And it is true that the motor-power of Imperialism is not chiefly financial: finance is rather the governor of the imperial engine, directing the energy and determining its work: it does not constitute the fuel of the engine, nor does it directly generate the power. Finance manipulates the patriotic forces which politicians, soldiers, philanthropists, and traders generate; the enthusiasm for expansion which issues from these sources, though strong and genuine, is irregular and blind; the financial interest has those qualities of concentration and clear-sighted calculation which are needed to set Imperialism to work. An ambitious statesman, a frontier soldier, an over-zealous missionary, a pushing trader, may suggest or even initiate a step of imperial expansion, may assist in educating patriotic public opinion to the urgent need of some fresh advance, but the final determination rests with the financial power. The direct influence exercised by great financial houses in "high politics" is supported by the control which they exercise over the body of public opinion through the Press, which, in every "civilised" country, is becoming more and more their obedient instrument. While the specifically financial newspaper imposes "facts" and "opinions" on the business classes, the general body of the Press comes more and more under the conscious or unconscious domination of financiers. The case of the

[5] This disastrous attempt by Cape Colony leaders (with some connivance in London) to help overthrow the government of the Transvaal in December, 1895, seriously exacerbated British-Boer relations. [Editor's note]

South African Press, whose agents and correspondents fanned the martial flames in this country, was one of open ownership on the part of South African financiers, and this policy of owning newspapers for the sake of manufacturing public opinion is common in the great European cities. In Berlin, Vienna, and Paris many of the influential newspapers are held by financial houses, which use them, not primarily to make direct profits out of them, but in order to put into the public mind beliefs and sentiments which will influence public policy and thus affect the money market. In Great Britain this policy has not gone so far, but the alliance with finance grows closer every year, either by financiers purchasing a controlling share of newspapers, or by newspaper proprietors being tempted into finance. Apart from the financial Press, and financial ownership of the general Press, the City notoriously exercises a subtle and abiding influence upon leading London newspapers, and through them upon the body of the provincial Press, while the entire dependence of the Press for its business profits upon its advertising columns involves a peculiar reluctance to oppose the organised financial classes with whom rests the control of so much advertising business. Add to this the natural sympathy with a sensational policy which a cheap Press always manifests, and it becomes evident that the Press is strongly biassed towards Imperialism, and lends itself with great facility to the suggestion of financial or political Imperialists who desire to work up patriotism for some new piece of expansion.

Such is the array of distinctively economic forces making for Imperialism, a large loose group of trades and professions seeking profitable business and lucrative employment from the expansion of military and civil services, from the expenditure on military operations, the opening up of new tracts of territory and trade with the same, and the provision of new capital which these operations require, all these finding their central guiding and directing force in the power of the general financier.

The play of these forces does not openly appear. They are essentially parasites upon patriotism, and they adapt themselves to its protecting colours. In the mouths of their representatives are noble phrases, expressive of their desire to extend the area of civilisation, to establish good government, promote Christianity, extirpate slavery, and elevate the lower races. Some of the business men who hold such language may entertain a genuine, though usually a vague, desire to accomplish these ends, but they are primarily engaged in business, and they are not unaware of the utility of the more unselfish forces in furthering their ends. Their true attitude of mind is expressed by Mr. Rhodes in his famous description of "Her Majesty's Flag" as "the greatest commercial asset in the world.". . .

THE ECONOMIC TAPROOT OF IMPERIALISM

No mere array of facts and figures adduced to illustrate the economic nature of the new Imperialism will suffice to dispel the popular delusion that the use of national force to secure new markets by annexing fresh tracts of territory is a sound and a necessary policy for an advanced industrial country like Great Britain. It has indeed been proved that recent annexations of tropical countries, procured at great expense, have furnished poor and precarious markets, that our aggregate trade with our colonial possessions is virtually stationary, and that our most profitable and progressive trade is with rival industrial nations, whose territories we have no desire to annex, whose markets we cannot force, and whose active antagonism we are provoking by our expansive policy.

But these arguments are not conclusive.

It is open to Imperialists to argue thus: "We must have markets for our growing manufactures, we must have new outlets for the investment of our surplus capital and for the energies of the adventurous surplus of our population: such expansion is a necessity of life to a nation with our great and growing powers of production. An ever larger share of our population is devoted to the manufactures and commerce of towns, and is thus dependent for life and work upon food and raw materials from foreign lands. In order to buy and pay for these things we must sell our goods abroad. During the first three-quarters of the century we could do so without difficulty by a natural expansion of commerce with continental nations and our colonies, all of which were far behind us in the main arts of manufacture and the carrying trades. So long as England held a virtual monopoly of the world markets for certain important classes of manufactured goods, Imperialism was unnecessary. During the last thirty years this manufacturing and trading supremacy has been greatly impaired: other nations, especially Germany, the United States, and Belgium, have advanced with great rapidity, and while they have not crushed or even stayed the increase of our external trade, their competition is making it more and more difficult to dispose of the full surplus of our manufactures at a profit. The encroachments made by these nations upon our old markets, even in our own possessions, make it most urgent that we should take energetic means to secure new markets. These new markets must lie in hitherto undeveloped countries, chiefly in the tropics, where vast populations live capable of growing economic needs which our manufacturers and merchants can supply. Our rivals are seizing and annexing territories for similar purposes, and when they have annexed them close them to our trade. The diplomacy and the arms of Great Britain must be used in order to compel the owners of the new markets to deal with us: and experience shows that the safest means of securing and developing such markets is by establishing 'protectorates' or by annexation. The present value of these markets must not be taken as a final test of the economy of such a policy; the process of educating civilised needs which we can supply is of necessity a gradual one, and the cost of such imperialism must be regarded as a capital outlay, the fruits of which posterity will reap. The new markets may not be large, but they form serviceable outlets for the overflow of our great textile and metal industries, and, when the vast Asiatic and African populations of the interior are reached, a rapid expansion of trade may be expected to result.

"Far larger and more important is the pressure of capital for external fields of investment. Moreover, while the manufacturer and trader are well content to trade with foreign nations, the tendency for investors to work towards the political annexation of countries which contain their more speculative investments is very powerful. Of the fact of this pressure of capital there can be no question. Large savings are made which cannot find any profitable investment in this country; they must find employment elsewhere, and it is to the advantage of the nation that they should be employed as largely as possible in lands where they can be utilised in opening up markets for British trade and employment for British enterprise.

"However costly, however perilous, this process of imperial expansion may be, it is necessary to the continued existence and progress of our nation; if we abandoned it we must be content to leave the development of the world to other nations, who will everywhere cut into our trade, and even impair our means of securing the food and raw materials we require to support our population. Imperialism is thus seen to be, not a choice, but a necessity."

The practical force of this economic argument in politics is strikingly illustrated by the recent history of the United States. Here is a country which suddenly breaks through a conservative policy, strongly held by both political parties, bound up with every popular instinct and tradition, and flings itself into a rapid imperial career for which it possesses neither the material nor the moral equipment, risking the principles and practices of liberty and equality by the establishment of militarism and the forcible subjugation of peoples which it cannot safely admit to the condition of American citizenship.

Is this a mere wild freak of spread-eaglism, a burst of political ambition on the part of a nation coming to a sudden realisation of its destiny? Not at all. The spirit of adventure, the American "mission of civilisation," are, as forces making for Imperialism, clearly subordinate to the driving force of the economic factor. . . .

. . . American Imperialism is the natural product of the economic pressure of a sudden advance of capitalism which cannot find occupation at home and needs foreign markets for goods and for investments.

The same needs exist in European countries, and, as is admitted, drive Governments along the same path. Over-production in the sense of an excessive manufacturing plant, and surplus capital which cannot find sound investments within the country, force Great Britain, Germany, Holland, France to place larger and larger portions of their economic resources outside the area of their present political domain, and then stimulate a policy of political expansion so as to take in the new areas. The economic sources of this movement are laid bare by periodic trade-depressions due to an inability of producers to find adequate and profitable markets for what they can produce. The Majority Report of the Commission upon the Depression of Trade in 1885 put the matter in a nutshell. "That, owing to the nature of the times, the demand for our commodities does not increase at the same rate as formerly; that our capacity for production is consequently in excess of our requirements, and could be considerably increased at short notice; that this is due partly to the competition of the capital which is being steadily accumulated in the country." The Minority Report

straightly imputes the condition of affairs to "over production." Germany is at the present time suffering severely from what is called a glut of capital and of manufacturing power: she must have new markets; her Consuls all over the world are "hustling" for trade; trading settlements are forced upon Asia Minor; in East and West Africa, in China and elsewhere the German Empire is impelled to a policy of colonisation and protectorates as outlets for German commercial energy.

Every improvement of methods of production, every concentration of ownership and control, seems to accentuate the tendency. As one nation after another enters the machine economy and adopts advanced industrial methods, it becomes more difficult for its manufacturers, merchants, and financiers to dispose profitably of their economic resources, and they are tempted more and more to use their Governments in order to secure for their particular use some distant undeveloped country by annexation and protection.

The process we may be told is inevitable, and so it seems upon a superficial inspection. Everywhere appear excessive powers of production, excessive capital in search of investment. It is admitted by all business men that the growth of the powers of production in their country exceeds the growth in consumption, that more goods can be produced than can be sold at a profit, and that more capital exists than can find remunerative investment.

It is this economic condition of affairs that forms the taproot of Imperialism. If the consuming public in this country raised its standard of consumption to keep pace with every rise of productive powers, there could be no excess of goods or capital clamorous to use Imperialism in order to find markets: foreign trade would indeed exist, but there would be no difficulty in exchanging a small surplus of our manufactures for the food and raw material we annually absorbed, and all the savings that we made could find employment, if we chose, in home industries. . . .

Moral and Sentimental Factors

I

Analysis of the actual course of modern Imperialism has laid bare the combination of economic and political forces which fashions it. These forces are traced to their sources in the selfish interests of certain industrial, financial, and professional classes, seeking private advantages out of a policy of imperial expansion, and using this same policy to protect them in their economic, political, and social privileges against the pressure of democracy. It remains to answer the question, "Why does Imperialism escape general recognition for the narrow, sordid thing it is?" Each nation, as it watches from outside the Imperialism of its neighbours, is not deceived; the selfish interests of political and commercial classes are seen plainly paramount in the direction of the policy. So every other European nation recognises the true outlines of British Imperialism and charges us with hypocrisy in feigning blindness. This charge is false; no nation sees its own shortcomings; the charge of hypocrisy is seldom justly brought against an individual, against a nation never. Frenchmen and Germans believe that our zeal in promoting foreign missions, putting down slavery, and in spreading the arts of civilisation is a false disguise conveniently assumed to cover naked national self-assertion. The actual case is somewhat different.

There exists in a considerable though not a large proportion of the British nation a genuine desire to spread Christianity among the heathen, to diminish the cruelty and other sufferings which they believe exist in countries less fortunate than their own, and to do good work about the world in the cause of humanity. Most of the churches contain a small body of men and women deeply, even passionately, interested in such work, and a much larger number whose sympathy, though weaker, is quite genuine. Ill-trained for the most part in psychology and history, these people believe that religion and other arts of civili-

sation are portable commodities which it is our duty to convey to the backward nations, and that a certain amount of compulsion is justified in pressing their benefits upon people too ignorant at once to recognise them.

Is it surprising that the selfish forces which direct Imperialism should utilise the protective colours of these disinterested movements? Imperialist politicians, soldiers, or company directors, who push a forward policy by portraying the cruelties of the African slave raids or the infamous tyranny of a Prempeh or a Thebaw,[6] or who open out a new field for missionary enterprise in China or the Soudan, do not deliberately and consciously work up these motives in order to incite the British public. They simply and instinctively attach to themselves any strong, genuine elevated feeling which is of service, fan it and feed it until it assumes fervour, and utilise it for their ends. The politician always, the business man not seldom, believes that high motives qualify the political or financial benefits he gets: it is certain that Lord Salisbury[7] really believes that the South African war, for which his Government is responsible, has been undertaken for the benefit of the people of South Africa and will result in increased liberty and happiness; it is quite likely that Earl Grey[8] thinks that the Chartered Company which he directs is animated by a desire to improve the material and moral condition of the natives of Rhodesia and that it is attaining this object.

---

[6] Prempeh: Asantehene (leading chief) of the Ashanti in West Africa. Thebaw (or Thibaw): last king of Burma (deposed 1885). Both men were well-known opponents of the British in the late nineteenth century. [Editor's note]

[7] Salisbury: British prime minister in 1885–86, 1886–92, and 1896–1902. [Editor's note]

[8] Earl Grey: British Statesman (Governor-General of Canada, 1904–11) and, for a time, member of the board of directors of the British South Africa Company and administrator of Rhodesia. Not to be confused with his cousin, Sir Edward Grey: foreign secretary, 1905–16. [Editor's note]

So Leopold, King of the Belgians, has claimed for his government of the Congo — "Our only programme is that of the moral and material regeneration of the country." It is difficult to set any limit upon the capacity of men to deceive themselves as to the relative strength and worth of the motives which affect them: politicians, in particular, acquire so strong a habit of setting their projects in the most favourable light that they soon convince themselves that the finest result which they think may conceivably accrue from any policy is the actual motive of that policy. As for the public, it is only natural that it should be deceived. All the purer and more elevated adjuncts of Imperialism are kept to the fore by religious and philanthropic agencies: patriotism appeals to the general lust of power within a people by suggestions of nobler uses, adopting the forms of self-sacrifice to cover domination and the love of adventure. So Christianity becomes "imperialist" to the Archbishop of Canterbury, a "going out to all the world to preach the gospel"; trade becomes "imperialist" in the eyes of merchants seeking a world market.

It is precisely in this falsification of the real import of motives that the gravest vice and the most signal peril of Imperialism reside. When, out of a medley of mixed motives, the least potent is selected for public prominence because it is the most presentable, when issues of a policy which was not present at all to the minds of those who formed this policy are treated as chief causes, the moral currency of the nation is debased. The whole policy of Imperialism is riddled with this deception. Although no candid student of history will maintain for a moment that the entrance of British power into India, and the chief steps leading to the present British Empire there, were motived by considerations other than our own political and commercial aggrandisement, nothing is more common than to hear the gains which it is alleged the natives of the country have received from British rule assigned as the moral justification of our Indian Empire. The case of

Egypt is a still more striking one. Though the reasons openly assigned for the British occupation of Egypt were military and financial ones affecting our own interests, it is now commonly maintained that we went there in order to bestow the benefits which Egyptians have received from our sway, and that it would be positively wicked of us to keep the pledge we gave to withdraw within a short term of years from the country. When the ordinary Englishman reads how "at no previous period of his history has the fellah lived under a Government so careful to promote his interests or to preserve his rights," he instinctively exclaims, "Yes, that is what we went to Egypt for," though, in point of fact, the play of "Imperialism" which carried us there was determined by quite other considerations. Even if one supposes that the visible misgovernment of Egypt, in its bearing on the life of the inhabitants, did impart some unselfish element to our conduct, no one would suggest that as an operative force in the direction of our imperial policy such motive has ever determined our actions. Not even the most flamboyant Imperialist contends that England is a knight-errant, everywhere in search of a quest to deliver oppressed peoples from oppressive governments, regardless of her own interests and perils. Though perhaps not so inefficient, the Russian tyranny is quite as oppressive and more injurious to the cause of civilisation than the government of the Khedive,[9] but no one proposes that we should coerce Russia, or rescue Finland from her clutches. The case of Armenia, again, attests the utter feebleness of the higher motives. Both the Government and the people of Great Britain were thoroughly convinced of the atrocious cruelties of Turkey, public opinion was well informed and thoroughly incensed, Great Britain was expressly pledged by the Cyprus Convention to protect Armenia; but the "cause of humanity" and the "mis-

[9] Khedive: title of Turkish viceroys in Egypt, after 1867. [Editor's note]

sion of civilisation" were powerless either for interference or for effective protest. . . .

III

. . . The controlling and directing agent of the whole process, as we have seen, is the pressure of financial and industrial motives, operated for the direct, short-range, material interests of small, able, and well-organised groups in a nation. These groups secure the active cooperation of statesmen and of political cliques who wield the power of "parties" partly by associating them directly in their business schemes, partly by appealing to the conservative instincts of members of the possessing classes, whose vested interests and class dominance are best preserved by diverting the currents of political energy from domestic on to foreign politics. The acquiescence, even the active and enthusiastic support, of the body of a nation in a course of policy fatal to its own true interests is secured partly by appeals to the mission of civilisation, but chiefly by playing upon the primitive instincts of the race.

The psychology of these instincts is not easy to explore, but certain prime factors easily appear. The passion which a French writer describes as kilometritis, or milomania, the instinct for control of land, drives back to the earliest times when a wide range of land was necessary for a food supply for men or cattle, and is linked on to the "trek" habit, which survives more powerfully than is commonly supposed in civilised peoples. The "nomadic" habit bred of necessity survives as a chief ingredient in the love of travel, and merges into "the spirit of adventure" when it meets other equally primitive passions. This "spirit of adventure," especially in the Anglo-Saxon, has taken the shape of "sport," which in its stronger or "more adventurous" forms involves a direct appeal to the lust of slaughter and the crude struggle for life involved in pursuit. The animal lust of struggle, once a necessity, survives in the blood, and just in proportion as a nation or a class has a margin of energy and leisure from the activities of peaceful industry, it craves satisfaction through "sport," in which hunting and the physical satisfaction of striking a blow are vital ingredients. The leisured classes in Great Britain, having most of their energy liberated from the necessity of work, naturally specialise on "sport," the hygienic necessity of a substitute for work helping to support or coalescing with the survival of a savage instinct. As the milder expressions of this passion are alone permissible in the sham or artificial encounters of domestic sports, where wild game disappears and human conflicts more mortal than football are prohibited, there is an ever stronger pressure to the frontiers of civilisation in order that the thwarted "spirit of adventure" may have strong, free play. These feelings are fed by a flood of the literature of travel and of imaginative writing, the security and monotony of the ordinary civilised routine imparting an ever-growing fascination to the wilder portions of the earth. The milder satisfactions afforded by sport to the upper classes in their ample leisure at home are imitated by the industrial masses, whose time and energy for recreation have been growing, and who, in their passage from rural to town conditions, have never abandoned the humbler sports of feudal country life to which from time immemorial they had been addicted. "Football is a good game, but better than it, better than any other game, is that of man-hunting."

The sporting and military aspects of Imperialism form, therefore, a very powerful basis of popular appeal. The desire to pursue and kill either big game or other men can only be satisfied by expansion and militarism. It may indeed be safely said that the reason why our army is so inefficient in its officers, as compared with its rank and file, is that at a time when serious scientific preparation and selection are required for an intellectual profession, most British officers choose the army and undertake its work in the spirit of "sport." While the average "Tommy" is perhaps actuated in the main by similar motives, "science" matters less in his case, and any lack of serious professional purpose is more largely compensated by the discipline imposed on him.

But still more important than these supports of militarism in the army is the part played by "war" as a support of Imperialism in the non-combatant body of the nation. Though the active appeal of "sport" is still strong, even among townsmen, clear signs are visible of a degradation of this active interest of the participant into the idle excitement of the spectator. How far sport has thus degenerated may be measured by the substitution everywhere of a specialised professionalism for a free amateur exercise, and by the growth of the attendant vice of gambling, which everywhere expresses the worst form of sporting excitement, drawing all disinterested sympathy away from the merits of the competition, and concentrating it upon the irrational element of chance in combination with covetousness and low cunning. The equivalent of this degradation of interest in sport is Jingoism in relation to the practice of war. Jingoism is merely the lust of the spectator, unpurged by any personal effort, risk, or sacrifice, gloating in the perils, pains, and slaughter of fellow-men whom he does not know, but whose destruction he desires in a blind and artificially stimulated passion of hatred and revenge. In the Jingo all is concentrated on the hazard and blind fury of the fray. The arduous and weary monotony of the march, the long periods of waiting, the hard privations, the terrible tedium of a prolonged campaign, play no part in his imagination; the redeeming factors of war, the fine sense of comradeship which common personal peril educates, the fruits of discipline and self-restraint, the respect for the personality of enemies whose courage he must admit and whom he comes to realise as fellow-beings — all these moderating elements in actual war are eliminated from the passion of the Jingo. It is precisely for these reasons that some friends of peace maintain that the two most potent checks of militarism and of war are the obligation of the entire body of citizens to undergo

military service and the experience of an invasion.

Whether such expensive remedies are really effectual or necessary we are not called on to decide, but it is quite evident that the spectatorial lust of Jingoism is a most serious factor in Imperialism. The dramatic falsification both of war and of the whole policy of imperial expansion required to feed this popular passion forms no small portion of the art of the real organisers of imperialist exploits, the small groups of business men and politicians who know what they want and how to get it.

Tricked out with the real or sham glories of military heroism and the magnificent claims of empire-making, Jingoism becomes a nucleus of a sort of patriotism which can be moved to any folly or to any crime.

IV

Where this spirit of naked dominance needs more dressing for the educated classes of a nation, the requisite moral and intellectual decorations are woven for its use; the church, the press, the schools and colleges, the political machine, the four chief instruments of popular education, are accommodated to its service. From the muscular Christianity of the last generation to the imperial Christianity of the present day it is but a single step; the temper of growing sacerdotalism and the doctrine of authority in the established churches well accord with militarism and political autocracy. Mr. Goldwin Smith has rightly observed how "force is the natural ally of superstition, and superstition knows it well." As for the most potent engine of the press, the newspaper, so far as it is not directly owned and operated by financiers for financial purposes (as is the case to a great extent in every great industrial and financial centre), it is always influenced and mostly dominated by the interests of the classes which control the advertisements upon which its living depends; the independence of a paper with a circulation so large and firm as to "command" and to retain advertisements in the teeth of a policy disliked by the advertising classes is becoming rarer and more precarious every year, as the cluster of interests which form the business nucleus of Imperialism becomes more consolidated and more conscious in its politics. The political machine is an hireling, because it is a machine, and needs constant repair and lubrication from the wealthy members of the party; the machinist knows from whom he takes his pay, and cannot run against the will of those who are in fact the patrons of the party, the tightening of whose purse-strings will automatically stop the machine. The recent Imperialism both of Great Britain and America has been materially assisted by the lavish contributions of men like Rockefeller, Hanna, Rhodes, Beit to party funds for the election of "imperialist" representatives and for the political instruction of the people.

Most serious of all is the persistent attempt to seize the school system for Imperialism masquerading as patriotism. To capture the childhood of the country, to mechanise its free play into the routine of military drill, to cultivate the savage survivals of combativeness, to poison its early understanding of history by false ideals and pseudo-heroes and by a consequent disparagement and neglect of the really vital and elevating lessons of the past, to establish a "geocentric" view of the moral universe in which the interests of humanity are subordinated to that of the "country" (and so, by easy, early, natural inference, that of the "country" to that of the "self"), to feed the always overweening pride of race at an age when self-confidence most commonly prevails, and by necessary implication to disparage other nations, so starting children in the world with false measures of value and an unwillingness to learn from foreign sources — to fasten this base insularity of mind and morals upon the little children of a nation and to call it patriotism is as foul an abuse of education as it is possible to conceive. Yet the power of Church and State over primary education is being bent consistently to this purpose, while the

blend of clericalism and autocratic academicism which dominates the secondary education of this country pours its enthusiasm into the same evil channel. Finally, our centres of highest culture, the universities, are in peril of a new perversion from the path of free inquiry and expression, which is the true path of intellectual life. A new sort of "pious founder" threatens intellectual liberty. Our colleges are, indeed, no longer to be the subservient defenders of religious orthodoxy, repressing science, distorting history, and moulding philosophy to conserve the interests of Church and King. The academic studies and their teachers are to employ the same methods, but directed to a different end: philosophy, the natural sciences, history, economics, sociology, are to be employed in setting up new earthworks against the attack of the disinherited masses upon the vested interests of the plutocracy. I do not of course represent this perversion as destructive of the educational work of the colleges: the services rendered in defence of "conservatism" may even be regarded in most cases as incidental: only perhaps in philosophy and economics is the bias a powerful and pervasive one, and even there the individuality of strong independent natures may correct it. Moreover, it is needless to charge dishonesty against the teachers, who commonly think and teach according to the highest that is in them. But the actual teaching is none the less selected and controlled, wherever it is found useful to employ the arts of selection and control, by the business interests playing on the vested academic interests. No one can follow the history of political and economic theory during the last century without recognising that the selection and rejection of ideas, hypotheses, and formulæ, the moulding of them into schools or tendencies of thought, and the propagation of them in the intellectual world, have been plainly directed by the pressure of class interests. In political economy, as we might well suspect, from its close bearing upon business and politics, we find the most incontestable example.

The "classical" economics in England were the barely disguised formulation of the mercantile and manufacturing interests as distinguished from, and opposed to, the landowning interest on the one hand, the labouring interest on the other, evoking in later years other class economics of "protection" and of "socialism" similarly woven out of sectional interests.

The real determinants in education are given in these three questions: "Who shall teach? What shall they teach? How shall they teach?" Where universities are dependent for endowments and incomes upon the favour of the rich, upon the charity of millionaires, the following answers will of necessity be given: "Safe teachers. Safe studies. Sound (*i.e.* orthodox) methods." The coarse proverb which tells us that "he who pays the piper calls the tune" is quite as applicable here as elsewhere, and no bluff regarding academic dignity and intellectual honesty must blind us to the fact.

The interference with intellectual liberty is seldom direct, seldom personal, though of late both in the United States and Canada some instances of the crudest heresy-hunting have occurred. The real danger consists in the appointment rather than in the dismissal of teachers, in the determination of what subjects shall be taught, what relative attention shall be given to each subject, and what text-books and other apparatus of instruction shall be used. The subservience to rank and money, even in our older English universities, has been of late evinced so nakedly, and the demands for monetary aid in developing new faculties necessarily looms so large in academic eyes, that the danger here indicated is an ever-growing one. It is not so much the weight of the "dead hand" that is to be feared as that of the living: a college so unfortunate as to harbour teachers who, in handling vital issues of politics or economics, teach truths deeply and obviously antagonistic to the interests of the classes from whom financial aid was sought, would be committing suicide. Higher education has never been economically self-supporting; it

has hardly ever been fully organised from public funds; everywhere it has remained parasitic on the private munificence of wealthy persons. The peril is too obvious to need further enforcement: it is the hand of the prospective, the potential donor that fetters intellectual freedom in our colleges, and will do so more and more so long as the duty of organising public higher education for a nation out of public funds fails of recognition.

The area of danger is, of course, far wider than Imperialism, covering the whole field of vested interests. But, if the analysis of previous chapters is correct, Imperialism stands as a first defence of these interests: for the financial and speculative classes it means a pushing of their private businesses at the public expense, for the export manufacturers and merchants a forcible enlargement of foreign markets and a related policy of Protection, for the official and professional classes large openings of honourable and lucrative employment, for the Church it represents the temper and practice of authority and the assertion of spiritual control over vast multitudes of lower people, for the political oligarchy it means the only effective diversion of the forces of democracy and the opening of great public careers in the showy work of empire-making.

This being so, it is inevitable that Imperialism should seek intellectual support in our seats of learning, and should use the sinews of education for the purpose. The millionaire who endows Oxford does not buy its men of learning outright, need not even stipulate what should be taught. But the practical pressure of Imperialism is such that when a professional appointment is made in history it is becoming more difficult for a scholar with the intellectual outlook of a John Morley, a Frederick Harrison, or a Goldwin Smith to secure election, or for a political economist with strong views on the necessity of controlling capital to be elected to a chair in economics. No formal tests are necessary; the instinct of financial self-preservation will suffice. The price which universities pay for preferring money and social position to intellectual distinction in the choice of chancellors and for touting among the millionaires for the equipment of new scientific schools is this subservience to the political and business interests of their patrons: their philosophy, their history, their economics, even their biology must reflect in doctrine and method the consideration that is due to patronage, and the fact that this deference is unconscious enhances the damage done to the cause of intellectual freedom.

Thus do the industrial and financial forces of Imperialism, operating through the party, the press, the church, the school, mould public opinion and public policy by the false idealisation of those primitive lusts of struggle, domination, and acquisitiveness which have survived throughout the eras of peaceful industrial order and whose stimulation is needed once again for the work of imperial aggression, expansion, and the forceful exploitation of lower races. For these business politicians biology and sociology weave thin convenient theories of a race struggle for the subjugation of the inferior peoples, in order that we, the Anglo-Saxon, may take their lands and live

upon their labours; while economics buttresses the argument by representing our work in conquering and ruling them as our share in the division of labour among nations, and history devises reasons why the lessons of past empire do not apply to ours, while social ethics paints the motive of "Imperialism" as the desire to bear the "burden" of educating and elevating races of "children." Thus are the "cultured" or semi-cultured classes indoctrinated with the intellectual and moral grandeur of Imperialism. For the masses there is a cruder appeal to hero-worship and sensational glory, adventure and the sporting spirit: current history falsified in coarse flaring colours, for the direct stimulation of the combative instincts. But while various methods are employed, some delicate and indirect, others coarse and flamboyant, the operation everywhere resolves itself into an incitation and direction of the brute lusts of human domination which are everywhere latent in civilised humanity, for the pursuance of a policy fraught with material gain to a minority of co-operative vested interests which usurp the title of the commonwealth.

THE HIGHEST STAGE OF CAPITALISM

V. I. LENIN

The Communist leader of the Russian Revolution, V. I. Lenin (1870–1924), wrote *Imperialism. The Highest Stage of Capitalism* while still in exile in Switzerland in 1916. It has been argued that he was probably motivated in this more by a desire to justify certain of his political programs and activities than to present a balanced analysis of contemporary European expansion—though certainly many writers have also argued that he did achieve the latter. The work is extremely theoretical. Lenin claimed, later, that he had been unable to be as specific and explicit on political matters as he could have been had the essay been written after he achieved power. As it was, he relied to a great extent on the theoretical position of the great Austrian-trained economist, Rudolph Hilferding, and on Hobson. Much of the text is made up of criticism of the writings of Karl Kautsky, a fellow Marxist who, as a late convert to a more moderate point of view than Lenin's, was one of the "opportunists" whose position Lenin was always trying to destroy.

THE DIVISION OF THE WORLD AMONG THE GREAT POWERS

IN his book, *The Territorial Development of the European Colonies*, A. Supan, the geographer, gives the following brief summary of this development at the end of the nineteenth century:

PERCENTAGE OF TERRITORIES BELONGING TO
THE EUROPEAN COLONIAL POWERS
(*Including United States*)

	1876	1900	Increase or Decrease
Africa	10.8	90.4	+ 79.6
Polynesia	56.8	98.9	+ 42.1
Asia	51.5	56.6	+ 5.1
Australia	100.0	100.0	...
America	27.5	27.2	− 0.3

"The characteristic feature of this period," he concludes, "is, therefore, the division of Africa and Polynesia."

As there are no unoccupied territories — that is, territories that do not belong to any state — in Asia and America, Mr. Supan's conclusion must be carried further, and we must say that the characteristic feature of this period is the final partition of the globe — not in the sense that a *new* partition is impossible — on the contrary, new partitions are possible and inevitable — but in the sense that the colonial policy of the capitalist countries has *completed* the seizure of the unoccupied territories on our planet. For the first time the world is completely divided up, so that in the future *only* redivision is possible; territories can only pass from one "owner" to another, instead of passing as unowned territory to an "owner."

Hence, we are passing through a peculiar period of world colonial policy, which is closely associated with the "latest stage in the development of capitalism," with finance

From V. I. Lenin, *Imperialism. The Highest Stage of Capitalism*, new, revised translation (New York, 1939), pp. 76–84, 88–92, 123–127. By permission of the International Publishers Co., Inc.

29

capital. For this reason, it is essential first of all to deal in detail with the facts, in order to ascertain exactly what distinguishes this period from those preceding it, and what the present situation is. In the first place, two questions of fact arise here. Is an intensification of colonial policy, an intensification of the struggle for colonies, observed precisely in this period of finance capital? And how, in this respect, is the world divided at the present time?

The American writer, Morris, in his book on the history of colonisation, has made an attempt to compile data on the colonial possessions of Great Britain, France and Germany during different periods of the nineteenth century. The following is a brief summary of the results he has obtained:

COLONIAL POSSESSIONS
(Million square miles and million inhabitants)

	Great Britain		France		Germany	
	Area	Pop.	Area	Pop.	Area	Pop.
1815–30	?	126.4	0.02	0.5	...	...
1860	2.5	145.1	0.2	3.4	...	...
1880	7.7	267.9	0.7	7.5	...	...
1899	9.3	309.0	3.7	56.4	1.0	14.7

For Great Britain, the period of the enormous expansion of colonial conquests is that between 1860 and 1880, and it was also very considerable in the last twenty years of the nineteenth century. For France and Germany this period falls precisely in these last twenty years. We saw above that the apex of pre-monopoly capitalist development, of capitalism in which free competition was predominant, was reached in the 'sixties and 'seventies of the last century. We now see that it is *precisely after that period* that the "boom" in colonial annexations begins, and that the struggle for the territorial division of the world becomes extraordinarily keen. It is beyond doubt, therefore, that capitalism's transition to the stage of monopoly capitalism, to finance capital, is *bound up* with the intensification of the struggle for the partition of the world.

Hobson, in his work on imperialism, marks the years 1884–1900 as the period of the intensification of the colonial "expansion" of the chief European states. According to his estimate, Great Britain during these years acquired 3,700,000 square miles of territory with a population of 57,000,000; France acquired 3,600,000 square miles with a population of 36,500,000; Germany 1,000,000 square miles with a population of 16,700,000; Belgium 900,000 square miles with 30,000,000 inhabitants; Portugal 800,000 square miles with 9,000,000 inhabitants. The quest for colonies by all the capitalist states at the end of the nineteenth century and particularly since the 1880's is a commonly known fact in the history of diplomacy and of foreign affairs.

When free competition in Great Britain was at its zenith, *i.e.*, between 1840 and 1860, the leading British bourgeois politicians were opposed to colonial policy and were of the opinion that the liberation of the colonies and their complete separation from Britain was inevitable and desirable. M. Beer, in an article, "Modern British Imperialism," published in 1898, shows that in 1852, Disraeli, a statesman generally inclined towards imperialism, declared: "The colonies are millstones round our necks." But at the end of the nineteenth century the heroes of the hour in England were Cecil Rhodes and Joseph Chamberlain, open advocates of imperialism, who applied the imperialist policy in the most cynical manner.

It is not without interest to observe that even at that time these leading British bourgeois politicians fully appreciated the connection between what might be called the purely economic and the politico-social roots of modern imperialism. Chamberlain advocated imperialism by calling it a "true, wise and economical policy," and he pointed particularly to the German, American and Belgian competition which Great Britain was encountering in the world market. Salvation lies in monopolies, said the capitalists as they formed cartels, syndicates and trusts. Salvation lies in monopolies, echoed the political leaders of the bourgeoisie, hastening to appropriate the parts of the world not yet shared out. The journalist, Stead, relates the following remarks uttered by his close friend Cecil Rhodes, in 1895, regarding his imperialist ideas:

I was in the East End of London yesterday and attended a meeting of the unemployed. I listened to the wild speeches, which were just a cry for "bread," "bread," "bread," and on my way home I pondered over the scene and I became more than ever convinced of the importance of imperialism. . . . My cherished idea is a solution for the social problem, *i.e.*, in order to save the 40,000,000 inhabitants of the United Kingdom from a bloody civil war, we colonial statesmen must acquire new lands to settle the surplus population, to provide new markets for the goods produced by them in the factories and mines. The Empire, as I have always said, is a bread and butter question. If you want to avoid civil war, you must become imperialists.

This is what Cecil Rhodes, millionaire, king of finance, the man who was mainly responsible for the Boer War, said in 1895. His defence of imperialism is just crude and cynical, but in substance it does not differ from the "theory" advocated by Messrs. Maslov, Südekum, Potresov, David, and the founder of Russian Marxism and others. Cecil Rhodes was a somewhat more honest social-chauvinist.

To tabulate as exactly as possible the territorial division of the world, and the changes which have occurred during the last decades, we will take the data furnished by Supan in the work already quoted on the colonial possessions of all the powers of the world. Supan examines the years 1876 and 1900; we will take the year 1876 — a year aptly selected, for it is precisely at that time that the pre-monopolist stage of development of West European capitalism can be said to have been completed, in the main, and we will take the year 1914, and in place of Supan's figures we will quote the more recent statistics of Hübner's *Geographical and Statistical Tables*. Supan gives figures only for colonies: we think it useful in order to present a complete picture of the division of the world to add brief figures on non-colonial and semi-colonial countries like Persia, China and Turkey. Persia is already almost completely a colony; China and Turkey are on the way to becoming colonies. We thus get the following summary:

COLONIAL POSSESSIONS OF THE GREAT POWERS
(Million square kilometers and million inhabitants)

	Colonies				Home Countries		Total	
	1876		1914		1914		1914	
	Area	Pop.	Area	Pop.	Area	Pop.	Area	Pop.
Great Britain	22.5	251.9	33.5	393.5	0.3	46.5	33.8	440.0
Russia	17.0	15.9	17.4	33.2	5.4	136.2	22.8	169.4
France	0.9	6.0	10.6	55.5	0.5	39.6	11.1	95.1
Germany	...	...	2.9	12.3	0.5	64.9	3.4	77.2
U.S.A.	...	...	0.3	9.7	9.4	97.0	9.7	106.7
Japan	...	...	0.3	19.2	0.4	53.0	0.7	72.2
Total	40.4	273.8	65.0	523.4	16.5	437.2	81.5	960.6
Colonies of other powers (Belgium, Holland, etc.)							9.9	45.3
Semi-colonial countries (Persia, China, Turkey)							14.5	361.2
Other countries							28.0	289.9
Total area and population of the world							133.9	1,657.0

We see from these figures how "complete" was the partition of the world at the end of the nineteenth and beginning of the twentieth centuries. After 1876 colonial possessions increased to an enormous degree, more than one and a half times, from 40,000,000 to 65,000,000 square kilometres in area for the six biggest powers, an increase of 25,000,000 square kilometres, that is, one and a half times greater than the area of the "home" countries, which have a total of 16,500,000 square kilometres. In 1876 three powers had no colonies, and a fourth, France, had scarcely any. In 1914 these four powers had 14,100,000 square kilometres of colonies, or an area one and a half times greater than that of Europe, with a population of nearly 100,000,000. The unevenness in the rate of expansion of colonial possessions is very marked. If, for instance, we compare France, Germany and Japan, which do not differ very much in area and population, we will see that the first has annexed almost three times as much colonial territory as the other two combined. In regard to finance capital, also, France, at the beginning of the period we are considering, was perhaps several times richer than Germany and Japan put together. In addition to, and on the basis of, purely economic causes, geographical conditions and other factors also affect the dimensions of colonial possessions. However strong the process of levelling the world, of levelling the economic and living conditions in different countries, may have been in the past decades as a result of the pressure of large-scale industry, exchange and finance capital, great differences still remain; and among the six powers, we see, firstly, young capitalist powers (America, Germany, Japan) which progressed very rapidly; secondly, countries with an old capitalist development (France and Great Britain), which, of late, have made much slower progress than the previously mentioned countries, and, thirdly, a country (Russia) which is economically most backward, in which modern capitalist imperialism is enmeshed, so to speak, in a particularly close network of pre-capitalist relations.

Alongside the colonial possessions of these great powers, we have placed the small colonies of the small states, which are, so to speak, the next possible and probable objects of a new colonial "shareout." Most of these little states are able to retain their colonies only because of the conflicting interests, frictions, etc., among the big powers, which prevent them from coming to an agreement in regard to the division of the spoils. The "semi-colonial states" provide an example of the transitional forms which are to be found in all spheres of nature and society. Finance capital is such a great, it may be said, such a decisive force in all economic and international relations, that it is capable of subordinating to itself, and actually does subordinate to itself, even states enjoying complete political independence. We shall shortly see examples of this. Naturally, however, finance capital finds it most "convenient," and is able to extract the greatest profit from a subordination which involves the loss of the political independence of the subjected countries and peoples. In this connection, the semi-colonial countries provide a typical example of the "middle stage." It is natural that the struggle for these semi-dependent countries should have become particularly bitter during the period of finance capital, when the rest of the world had already been divided up.

Colonial policy and imperialism existed before this latest stage of capitalism, and even before capitalism. Rome, founded on slavery, pursued a colonial policy and achieved imperialism. But "general" arguments about imperialism, which ignore, or put into the background the fundamental difference of social-economic systems, inevitably degenerate into absolutely empty banalities, or into grandiloquent comparisons like "Greater Rome and Greater Britain." Even the colonial policy of capitalism in its *previous* stages is essentially different from the colonial policy of finance capital.

The principal feature of modern capitalism is the domination of monopolist combines of the big capitalists. These monopolies are most firmly established when *all* the sources of raw materials are controlled by the one group. And we have seen with what zeal the international capitalist combines exert every effort to make it impossible for their rivals to compete with them; for example, by buying up

mineral lands, oil fields, etc. Colonial possession alone gives complete guarantee of success to the monopolies against all the risks of the struggle with competitors, including the risk that the latter will defend themselves by means of a law establishing a state monopoly. The more capitalism is developed, the more the need for raw materials is felt, the more bitter competition becomes, and the more feverishly the hunt for raw materials proceeds throughout the whole world, the more desperate becomes the struggle for the acquisition of colonies.

Schilder writes:

It may even be asserted, although it may sound paradoxical to some, that in the more or less discernible future the growth of the urban industrial population is more likely to be hindered by a shortage of raw materials for industry than by a shortage of food.

For example, there is a growing shortage of timber — the price of which is steadily rising — of leather, and raw materials for the textile industry.

As instances of the efforts of associations of manufacturers to create an equilibrium between industry and agriculture in world economy as a whole, we might mention the International Federation of Cotton Spinners' Associations in the most important industrial countries, founded in 1904, and the European Federation of Flax Spinners' Associations, founded on the same model in 1910.

The bourgeois reformists, and among them particularly the present-day adherents of Kautsky, of course, try to belittle the importance of facts of this kind by arguing that it "would be possible" to obtain raw materials in the open market without a "costly and dangerous" colonial policy; and that it would be "possible" to increase the supply of raw materials to an enormous extent "simply" by improving agriculture. But these arguments are merely an apology for imperialism, an attempt to embellish it, because they ignore the principal feature of modern capitalism: monopoly. Free markets are becoming more and more a thing of the past; monopolist syndicates and trusts are restricting them more and more every day, and "simply" improving agriculture reduces itself to improving the conditions of the masses, to raising wages and reducing profits. Where, except in the imagination of the sentimental reformists, are there any trusts capable of interesting themselves in the condition of the masses instead of the conquest of colonies?

Finance capital is not only interested in the already known sources of raw materials; it is also interested in potential sources of raw materials, because present-day technical development is extremely rapid, and because land which is useless today may be made fertile tomorrow if new methods are applied (to devise these new methods a big bank can equip a whole expedition of engineers, agricultural experts, etc.), and large amounts of capital are invested. This also applies to prospecting for minerals, to new methods of working up and utilising raw materials, etc., etc. Hence, the inevitable striving of finance capital to extend its economic territory and even its territory in general. In the same way that the trusts capitalise their property by estimating it at two or three times its value, taking into account its "potential" (and not present) returns, and the further results of monopoly, so finance capital strives to seize the largest possible amount of land of all kinds and in any place it can, and by any means, counting on the possibilities of finding raw materials there, and fearing to be left behind in the insensate struggle for the last available scraps of undivided territory, or for the repartition of that which has been already divided.

The British capitalists are exerting every effort to develop cotton growing in *their* colony, Egypt (in 1904, out of 2,300,000 hectares of land under cultivation, 600,000, or more than one-fourth, were devoted to cotton growing); the Russians are doing the same in *their* colony, Turkestan; and they are doing so because in this way they will be in a better position to defeat their foreign competitors, to monopolise the sources of raw materials and form a more economical and profitable textile trust in which *all* the processes of cotton production and manufacturing will be "combined" and concentrated in the hands of a single owner.

The necessity of exporting capital also gives an impetus to the conquest of colonies, for in the colonial market it is easier to eliminate competition, to make sure of orders, to strengthen the necessary "connections," etc., by monopolist methods (and sometimes it is the only possible way). . . .

IMPERIALISM AS A SPECIAL STAGE OF CAPITALISM

We must now try to sum up and put together what has been said above on the subject of imperialism. Imperialism emerged as the development and direct continuation of the fundamental attributes of capitalism in general. But capitalism only became capitalist imperialism at a definite and very high stage of its development, when certain of its fundamental attributes began to be transformed into their opposites, when the features of a period of transition from capitalism to a higher social and economic system began to take shape and reveal themselves all along the line. Economically, the main thing in this process is the substitution of capitalist monopolies for capitalist free competition. Free competition is the fundamental attribute of capitalism, and of commodity production generally. Monopoly is exactly the opposite of free competition; but we have seen the latter being transformed into monopoly before our very eyes, creating large-scale industry and eliminating small industry, replacing large-scale industry by still larger-scale industry, finally leading to such a concentration of production and capital that monopoly has been and is the result:

cartels, syndicates and trusts, and merging with them, the capital of a dozen or so banks manipulating thousands of millions. At the same time monopoly, which has grown out of free competition, does not abolish the latter, but exists over it and alongside of it, and thereby gives rise to a number of very acute, intense antagonisms, friction and conflicts. Monopoly is the transition from capitalism to a higher system.

If it were necessary to give the briefest possible definition of imperialism we should have to say that imperialism is the monopoly stage of capitalism. Such a definition would include what is most important, for, on the one hand, finance capital is the bank capital of a few big monopolist banks, merged with the capital of the monopolist combines of manufacturers; and, on the other hand, the division of the world is the transition from a colonial policy which has extended without hindrance to territories unoccupied by any capitalist power, to a colonial policy of monopolistic possession of the territory of the world which has been completely divided up.

But very brief definitions, although convenient, for they sum up the main points, are nevertheless inadequate, because very important features of the phenomenon that has to be defined have to be especially deduced. And so, without forgetting the conditional and relative value of all definitions, which can never include all the concatenations of a phenomenon in its complete development, we must give a definition of imperialism that will embrace the following five essential features:

1) The concentration of production and capital developed to such a high stage that it created monopolies which play a decisive role in economic life.

2) The merging of bank capital with industrial capital, and the creation, on the basis of this "finance capital," of a "financial oligarchy."

3) The export of capital, which has become extremely important, as distinguished from the export of commodities.

4) The formation of international capitalist monopolies which share the world among themselves.

5) The territorial division of the whole world among the greatest capitalist powers is completed.

Imperialism is capitalism in that stage of development in which the dominance of monopolies and finance capital has established itself; in which the export of capital has acquired pronounced importance; in which the division of the world among the international trusts has begun; in which the division of all territories of the globe among the great capitalist powers has been completed.

We shall see later that imperialism can and must be defined differently if consideration is to be given, not only to the basic, purely economic factors — to which the above definition is limited — but also to the historical place of this stage of capitalism in relation to capitalism in general, or to the relations between imperialism and the two main trends in the working class movement. The point to be noted just now is that imperialism, as interpreted above, undoubtedly represents a special stage in the development of capitalism. In order to enable the reader to obtain as well grounded an idea of imperialism as possible, we deliberately quoted largely from *bourgeois* economists who are obliged to admit the particularly incontrovertible facts regarding modern capitalist economy. With the same object in view, we have produced detailed statistics which reveal the extent to which bank capital, etc., has developed, showing how the transformation of quantity into quality, of developed capitalism into imperialism, has expressed itself. Needless to say, all boundaries in nature and in society are conditional and changeable, and, consequently, it would be absurd to discuss the exact year or the decade in which imperialism "definitely" became established.

In this matter of defining imperialism, however, we have to enter into controversy, primarily, with K. Kautsky, the principal Marxian theoretician of the epoch of the so-called Second International — that is, of the twenty-five years between 1889 and 1914.

Kautsky, in 1915 and even in November 1914, very emphatically attacked the fundamental ideas expressed in our definition of imperialism. Kautsky said that imperialism must not be regarded as a "phase" or stage of economy, but as a policy; a definite policy "preferred" by finance capital; that imperialism cannot be "identified" with "contemporary capitalism"; that if imperialism is to be understood to mean "all the phenomena of contemporary capitalism" — cartels, protection, the domination of the financiers and colonial policy — then the question as to whether imperialism is necessary to capitalism becomes reduced to the "flattest tautology"; because, in that case, "imperialism is naturally a vital necessity for capitalism," and so on. The best way to present Kautsky's ideas is to quote his own definition of imperialism, which is diametrically opposed to the substance of the ideas which we have set forth (for the objections coming from the camp of the German Marxists, who have been advocating such ideas for many years already, have been long known to Kautsky as the objections of a definite trend in Marxism).

Kautsky's definition is as follows:

Imperialism is a product of highly developed industrial capitalism. It consists in the striving of every industrial capitalist nation to bring under its control and to annex increasingly big *agrarian* [Kautsky's italics] regions irrespective of what nations inhabit those regions.

This definition is utterly worthless because it one-sidedly, *i.e.,* arbitrarily, brings out the national question alone (although this is extremely important in itself as well as in its relation to imperialism), it arbitrarily and *inaccurately* relates this question *only* to industrial capital in the countries which annex other nations, and in an equally arbitrary and inaccurate manner brings out the annexation of agrarian regions.

Imperialism is a striving for annexations — this is what the *political* part of Kautsky's definition amounts to. It is correct, but very incomplete, for politically, imperialism is, in general, a striving towards violence and reaction. For the moment, however, we are interested in the *economic* aspect of the question, which Kautsky *himself* introduced into *his* definition. The inaccuracy of Kautsky's definition is strikingly obvious. The characteristic feature of imperialism is *not* industrial capital, *but* finance capital. It is not an accident that in France it was precisely the extraordinarily rapid development of *finance* capital, and the weakening of industrial capital, that, from 1880 onwards, gave rise to the extreme extension of annexationist (colonial) policy. The characteristic feature of imperialism is precisely that it strives to annex *not only* agricultural regions, but even highly industrialised regions (German appetite for Belgium; French appetite for Lorraine), because 1) the fact that the world is already divided up obliges those contemplating a *new* division to reach out for *any kind* of territory, and 2) because an essential feature of imperialism is the rivalry between a number of great powers in the striving for hegemony, *i.e.,* for the conquest of territory, not so much directly for themselves as to weaken the adversary and undermine *his* hegemony. (Belgium is chiefly necessary to Germany as a base for operations against England; England needs Bagdad as a base for operations against Germany, etc.) . . .

THE PLACE OF IMPERIALISM IN HISTORY

We have seen that the economic quintessence of imperialism is monopoly capitalism. This very fact determines its place in history, for monopoly that grew up on the basis of free competition, and precisely out of free competition, is the transition from the capitalist system to a higher social-economic order. We must take special note of the four principal forms of monopoly, or the four principal manifestations of monopoly capitalism, which are characteristic of the epoch under review.

Firstly, monopoly arose out of the concentration of production at a very advanced stage of development. This refers to the monopolist capitalist combines, cartels, syndicates and trusts. We have seen the important part that these play in modern economic life. At the beginning of the twentieth century, monopolies acquired complete supremacy in the advanced countries. And although the first steps towards the formation of the cartels were first taken by countries enjoying the protection of high tariffs (Germany, America), Great Britain, with her system of free trade, was not far behind in revealing the same basic phenomenon, namely, the birth of monopoly out of the concentration of production.

Secondly, monopolies have accelerated the capture of the most important sources of raw materials, especially for the coal and iron industries, which are the basic and most highly cartelised industries in capitalist society. The monopoly of the most important sources of raw materials has enormously increased the power of big capital, and has sharpened the antagonism between cartelised and non-cartelised industry.

Thirdly, monopoly has sprung from the banks. The banks have developed from modest intermediary enterprises into the monopolists of finance capital. Some three or five of the biggest banks in each of the foremost capitalist countries have achieved the "personal union" of industrial and bank capital, and have concentrated in their hands the disposal of thousands upon thousands of millions which form the greater part of the capital and income of entire countries. A financial oligarchy, which throws a close net of relations of dependence over all the economic and political institutions of contemporary bourgeois society without exception — such is the most striking manifestation of this monopoly.

Fourthly, monopoly has grown out of colonial policy. To the numerous "old" motives of colonial policy, finance capital has added the struggle for the sources of raw materials, for the export of capital, for "spheres of influence," *i.e.*, for spheres for profitable deals, concessions, monopolist profits and so on; in fine, for economic territory in general. When the colonies of the European powers in Africa, for instance, comprised only one-tenth of that territory (as was the case in 1876), colonial policy was able to develop by methods other than those of monopoly — by the "free grabbing" of territories, so to speak. But when nine-tenths of Africa had been seized (approximately by 1900), when the whole world had been divided up, there was inevitably ushered in a period of colonial monopoly and, consequently, a period of particularly intense struggle for the division and the redivision of the world.

The extent to which monopolist capital has intensified all the contradictions of capitalism is generally known. It is sufficient to mention the high cost of living and the oppression of the cartels. This intensification of contradictions constitutes the most powerful driving force of the transitional period of history, which began from the time of the definite victory of world finance capital.

Monopolies, oligarchy, the striving for domination instead of the striving for liberty, the exploitation of an increasing number of small or weak nations by an extremely small group of the richest or most powerful nations — all these have given birth to those distinctive characteristics of imperialism which compel us to define it as parasitic or decaying capitalism. More and more prominently there emerges, as one of the tendencies of imperialism, the creation of the "bondholding" (rentier) state, the usurer state, in which the bourgeoisie lives on the proceeds of capital exports and by "clipping coupons." It would be a mistake to believe that this tendency to decay precludes the possibility of the rapid growth of capitalism. It does not. In the epoch of imperialism, certain branches of industry, certain strata of the bourgeoisie and certain countries betray, to a more or less degree, one or other of these tendencies. On the whole, capitalism is growing far more rapidly than before. But this growth is not only becoming more and more uneven in general; its unevenness also manifests itself, in particular, in the decay of the countries which are richest in capital (such as England).

In regard to the rapidity of Germany's economic development, Riesser, the author of the book on the big German banks, states:

The progress of the preceding period (1848–70), which had not been exactly slow, stood in about the same ratio to the rapidity with which the whole of Germany's national economy, and with it German banking, progressed during this period (1870–1905) as the mail coach of the Holy Roman Empire of the German nation stood to the speed of the present-day automobile . . . which in whizzing past, it must be said, often endangers not only innocent pedestrians in its path, but also the occupants of the car.

In its turn, this finance capital which has grown so rapidly is not unwilling (precisely because it has grown so quickly) to pass on to a more "tranquil" possession of colonies which have to be seized — and not only by peaceful methods — from richer nations. In the United States, economic development in the last decades has been even more rapid than in Germany, and *for this very reason* the parasitic character of modern

American capitalism has stood out with particular prominence. On the other hand, a comparison of, say, the republican American bourgeoisie with the monarchist Japanese or German bourgeoisie shows that the most pronounced political distinctions diminish to an extreme degree in the epoch of imperialism — not because they are unimportant in general, but because in all these cases we are discussing a bourgeoisie which has definite features of parasitism.

The receipt of high monopoly profits by the capitalists in one of the numerous branches of industry, in one of numerous countries, etc., makes it economically possible for them to corrupt certain sections of the working class, and for a time a fairly considerable minority, and win them to the side of the bourgeoisie of a given industry or nation against all the others. The intensification of antagonisms between imperialist nations for the division of the world increases this striving. And so there is created that bond between imperialism and opportunism, which revealed itself first and most clearly in England, owing to the fact that certain features of imperialist development were observable there much earlier than in other countries. . . .

From all that has been said in this book on the economic nature of imperialism, it follows that we must define it as capitalism in transition, or, more precisely, as moribund capitalism. It is very instructive in this respect to note that the bourgeois economists, in describing modern capitalism, frequently employ terms like "interlocking," "absence of isolation," etc.; "in conformity with their functions and course of development," banks are "not purely private business enterprises; they are more and more outgrowing the sphere of purely private business regulation." And this very Riesser, who uttered the words just quoted, declares with all seriousness that the "prophecy" of the Marxists concerning "socialisation" has "not come true"! . . .

EMPIRE AND COMMERCE

LEONARD WOOLF

Leonard Sidney Woolf (1880–   ), the well-known author, editor, publisher (and husband of Virginia Woolf, the author), spent seven years of his early adulthood in the Ceylon Civil Service. Returning to England shortly before World War I, he became interested in socialism and joined the Fabian Society and the Labour Party. Thereafter he was editor of the *International Review*, literary editor of the British *Nation*, editor (1931–1959) of the *Political Quarterly*, and author of a variety of works on political and social subjects. Woolf argued that "imperialism," while not necessarily inevitable, had resulted in the recent past from the greed of capitalist businessmen and governments. His controversial *Empire and Commerce in Africa* is a detailed examination of the European penetration into Africa, based on a multitude of facts. Critics argue that these facts are highly selective and that the conclusions drawn from them are therefore unreliable; but Woolf argues that the facts are representative and speak for themselves.

I HAVE already given some proof of the assertion that Europe has almost universally accepted the principle of policy that the power of the State should be used upon the world outside the State for the economic purposes of the world within the State. Detailed proofs will occur again and again in the pages which follow. But one word is necessary here to many persons who will immediately dissent from this interpretation of the modern statesman's and citizen's view of State action. They will accuse us of placing the cart before the horse, of confusing means with ends. Modern policy, they will say, has aimed at economic ends, but only to use them as means for other and higher ends. Thus Mr. Arthur Greenwood in an excellent little book, designed to instruct the uninitiated in the problems of international relations, writes thus of Mr. Chamberlain's twentieth-century campaign for the reintroduction of a "Colonial system":[1]

And much of the flood of argument was used to show the free-traders, on the one hand, that they would be better off under a protective tariff, and the protectionists on the other that they were better off with the system of free imports. But Mr. Chamberlain's motive was political. Rightly or wrongly, he believed that fiscal charges were called for in what he considered to be the best interests of the nation and the Empire. The economic results were not to him ends in themselves, but means for the realization of imperial power and prestige. The tariff was an economic instrument to be wielded for political purposes, a weapon with which to gain state ends in the sphere of international politics.

There is in Mr. Greenwood's exposition an element of truth, but also an element of confusion. It is true that Mr. Chamberlain's motive for desiring Colonial Preference was political rather than economic, in the sense that he recommended it as a weapon or means for the realization of im-

[1] Joseph Chamberlain, British colonial secretary, 1895–1903, resigned that office to campaign for imperial preference. [Editor's note]

From Leonard Woolf, *Empire and Commerce in Africa. A Study in Economic Imperialism* (London, 1919?), pp. 16–19, 24–27, 31–38. Reprinted by permission of George Allen & Unwin Ltd.

perial power and prestige. But it is wrong to argue that, therefore, Mr. Chamberlain did not regard national economic interests as the ultimate ends of policy. The question is whether Mr. Chamberlain regarded "imperial power and prestige" as the ultimate ends of national policy, or whether he really looked upon them only as means for the realization of other and more important ends. Now statesmen and nations are not always logical, clear, or consistent in their desires and beliefs. It is the commonest thing for human beings to shirk or confuse the issue as to whether something which they desire and aim at is to them an ultimate end or merely valuable as the means for realizing some other end. The man who desires money as a means for the realization of leisure and pleasure ends as a miser who desires money because it is money. It is possible that the Chamberlain of 1904 had come to believe that "imperial power and prestige" were ends in themselves: certainly some of his fellow-imperialists in all countries, and particularly Germany, have written and spoken as if Empire was to be desired simply because it is Empire. But that was most certainly not the view of the Chamberlain of 1896, who told the leaders of the Empire's commerce assembled in London that "I believe that the toast of Empire would have carried with it all that is meant by Commerce and Empire, because, gentlemen, the Empire, to parody a celebrated expression, is commerce." Nor was it the opinion of the Chamberlain of 1894 who said to the people of Birmingham:

Give me the demand for more goods and then I will undertake to give plenty of employment in making the goods; and the only thing, in my opinion, that the Government can do in order to meet this great difficulty that we are considering is so to arrange its policy that every inducement shall be given to the demand; that new markets shall be created, and that old markets shall be effectually developed. You are aware that some of my opponents please themselves occasionally by finding names for me, and among

other names lately they have been calling me a Jingo. I am no more a Jingo than you are. But for the reasons and arguments I have put before you to-night, I am convinced that it is a necessity, as well as a duty, for us to uphold the dominion and empire which we now possess. For these reasons among others I would never lose the hold which we now have over our great Indian dependency — by far the greatest and most valuable of all the customers we have or ever shall have in this country. For the same reasons I approve of the continued occupation of Egypt; and for the same reasons I have urged upon this Government, and upon previous Governments, the necessity for using every legitimate opportunity to extend our influence and control in that great African continent which is now being opened up to civilization and to commerce.

The Chamberlain of 1894 and 1896, it will be observed, regarded imperial power and prestige as definite means to economic ends, the provision of markets and customers, because he held that commerce, not empire and prestige, was the greatest of political interests. It is possible, as I have said, that a nation or a man who begins by seeking Empire as a means to commerce may end by acquiring a taste for Empire "in itself," just as many persons who begin to drink beer as a means of quenching thirst end by acquiring a taste for beer "in itself." That, however, does not affect the truth of the generalization that the main and ultimate end of policy during the last fifty years has been economic interests, commercial, industrial, and financial. What I propose to do in this book is to examine the results of this view that the power and organization of the State should be used upon the world outside the State in order to promote the economic interests of the world inside the State. For that purpose it is unnecessary at present to say anything more about the ends of this international economic policy. In the modern world there is little, if any, difference of opinion over those ends. . . .

*   *   *

Between 1880 and 1914 the States of

Britain, France, and Germany each acquired an immense colonial empire outside Europe. These empires were empires in the literal sense of the word: they were founded by conquest, sometimes openly acknowledged, and sometimes disguised under various synonyms for civilization. The territories acquired were incorporated, usually against the wishes of their inhabitants, in the European State, and the inhabitants were subjected to the autocratic rule of the European State. The territory acquired by the British State in this way was about 3¼ million square miles, and the population subjected to its rule was about 46 million. The French State acquired 4 million square miles, and a population of over 50 million; the German State 1 million square miles, and a population of 15 million. The policy which led to the acquisition of this empire by Britain was the policy of Mr. Chamberlain and his followers. The motives have been sufficiently illustrated above from the declarations of Mr. Chamberlain himself. They were purely economic. In conquering the unexploited portions of Asia and Africa we were "pegging out claims for posterity," and the claims of posterity were for more markets. And the reasons which this school of policy gave for our "never losing the hold which we now have" over "our great Indian dependency" and over Egypt were the same, namely, the provision of markets and customers for the European citizens of the British State. Now, if we turn to France, we find that in that country, too, the creation of a colonial empire was the work of a political party with definite and imperial and colonial aims. A French writer upon colonial affairs, an imperialist, and a man of sound and moderate judgments, M. E. Fallot, has pointed out that the first colonial acquisitions of France after the revolution were not the result of any conscious plan: they were fortuitous and occasional, the acts of a Government to which the people remained indifferent. But it is not the same with the colonial policy of the Republic for which Gambetta, Jules Ferry, and

Barthélemy Saint-Hilaire[2] were responsible. That policy was the result of a political plan carefully studied, applied methodically in the face of great difficulties, and finally realized with complete success. Those who urged this "politique coloniale" upon the French people with such persistence and success gave as their reasons for the necessity of "expansion" precisely the same political motives as the imperialists of Britain. The ends of the French "politique coloniale" were mainly economic, and where the Englishmen made "provision for markets" in Asia and Africa the Frenchman talked of the necessity for colonies as "débouchés à nos produits." If anything, the economic nature of the new imperialism was recognized or admitted earlier in France than in Britain. This is shown by the motives for the French Tonkin expedition which was almost the prelude to the imperial activities of the Republic and which was the first act in the partition or domination of China for economic ends by European States. Jules Ferry, the minister responsible for this expedition, at the time repeatedly defended his action by urging that the possession of Tonkin would assure to the French the navigation of the Red River, and that, thanks to that magnificent natural highway ("magnifique voie naturelle") they would be able to penetrate into China and secure for themselves the commercial monopoly of the Western Provinces of China.

It is true that particularly between 1880 and 1890 the partisans of the "politique coloniale" put forward motives, which were not economic, for their imperialism. In those early days it was pointed out, for instance, that France had to carry out in Algeria her mission of civilization ("remplir notre mission civilisatrice"). But the desire for and belief in Europe's mission of civili-

2 Léon Gambetta, as president of the Chamber of Deputies, 1879–81, and premier, 1881–82, Jules Ferry, as premier, 1880–81 and 1883–85, and Jules Barthélemy Saint-Hilaire, as minister of foreign affairs, 1880–81, inaugurated France's late nineteenth-century expansion. [Editor's note]

zation in Asia and Africa rapidly lost its position as a motive for policy in the last decade of the century. . . . After 1890 it is extremely rare to find any authoritative imperialist recommending imperialism as a duty: the stress is laid upon economic necessity and commercial profit. Thus, even the Englishman, Sir F. D. Lugard, an expert in these matters — for he added an immense territory to the British Empire — writes in 1893 that "the scramble for Africa . . . was due to the growing commercial rivalry, which brought home to civilized nations the vital necessity of securing the only remaining fields for industrial enterprise and expansion." "It is well then to realise," he continues, "that it is for our advantage — and not alone at the dictates of duty — that we have undertaken responsibilities in East Africa. It is in order to foster the growth of the trade of this country, and to find an outlet for our manufactures and our surplus energy, that our far-seeing statesmen and our commercial men advocate colonial expansion. . . . I do not believe that in these days our national policy is based on motives of philanthropy only." And Sir F. D. Lugard shows what, in his view, were the relative importance of the "dictates of duty," the motives of philanthropy, and economic motives, by saying practically nothing more about duty and philanthropy, but devoting whole chapters to the economic advantages which the inhabitants of Britain will derive from the subjection of Uganda to the British State. So, too, when a well-known French writer has to sum up in 1904 the causes of the French "mouvement colonial," he forgets to mention the "mission civilisatrice," and puts it all down to "vital necessity," the universal competition, and the struggle for national existence. . . .

* * *

Nowhere . . . is the economic nature of modern imperialism shown more clearly than in the history of Germany. The German has a brutal habit of saying what he thinks, and of calling spades spades. In German trade is not a synonym for Christianity, nor finance for civilization. Already in the '70's German writers were insisting upon the necessity of colonies for the protection and fostering of German trade. Innumerable schemes were put forward in newspapers and books and pamphlets for founding colonies in every part of the world. This was part of the same current of beliefs and desires which was also gathering strength in France and Britain, and which finally burst out into the economic imperialism of the '80's in all three countries. It was only the passion of Germans for dotting their i's and crossing their t's which made the nature of their beliefs and desires plain in those early years. This kind of propaganda culminated in Fabri's well-known book, *Bedarf Deutschland der Kolonien?* which was published in 1879. Fabri[3] answered his question in the affirmative for economic reasons, and proposed the foundation of "Handelskolonien" in Samoa, New Guinea, North Borneo, Formosa, Madagascar, and Central Africa. A strong and definite German policy of economic imperialism sprang directly from Fabri and his book. The important thing to notice is that this policy was not only pressed upon the Government for economic reasons, but, as in the case of French and British imperialism, its chief support came from certain strong financial and commercial interests.

The close connection between colonial policy and commercial interests began in Germany even before Fabri. In 1871 a proposal was put about that Samoa should be taken as a naval station and colony. The proposal was certainly not unconnected with the large Hamburg firm of Godeffroy which "was all-powerful in Samoa." At that time the Government was indisposed to imperialist adventure, and nothing came of the idea beyond the visit of German warships and the signing of treaties with the natives in 1876, 1877, and 1879. But in

[3] Friedrich Fabri was a German mission administrator for over twenty years. [Editor's note]

1878 there was a development most significant of the future. The Godeffroy firm was in difficulties, and proposed or threatened to sell its interests to the London firm of Baring. The firm of Godeffroy was one of the earliest to realize that financial difficulties can be made the first stepping-stone towards Empire. The method of converting bankruptcy into lucrative imperialism has since become a commonplace of colonial policy, but this early example, though unsuccessful, is illuminating. Godeffroy appealed to German patriotism not to allow him to sell patriotically his interests in Samoa to a British firm. He looked to German patriots to invest five million marks in a German Trading and Plantation Company which would relieve him of his South Sea interests. But the security offered by Herr Godeffroy was insufficient to induce German patriotism to invest more than one million marks; and one million marks was insufficient to induce Herr Godeffroy's patriotism to part with his interests. He then conceived the idea of appealing to the patriotism of the German Government by floating a new Company to take over his interests, and of inducing the Government to guarantee a 4½ per cent dividend for twenty years. In this way the interests of Herr Godeffroy, of German trade and finance, and of imperialism, would be all promoted, and the financial difficulties of Herr Godeffroy would become the first stepping-stone to a German colony in Samoa. At that time the German Government was Bismarck, and Bismarck was by no means favourable to "colonial policies" and economic imperialism. But no man can be more resourceful than a patriotic financier in financial difficulties. Herr Godeffroy went to a well-known financier, von Hansemann, Director of the Diskontogesellschaft, who was a friend of Geheimrat von Kusserow of the German Foreign Office, and of the banker von Bleichröder, who was Bismarck's financial adviser. Herr Godeffroy talked von Hansemann over to his scheme; von Hansemann talked over the Geheimrat and the banker; the

Geheimrat and the banker talked over Bismarck. And Bismarck was talked over because Herr Godeffroy could, as it happened, offer a *quid pro quo*. At that moment Bismarck was anxious to get his protection proposals accepted among the trading interests, particularly in the Hanse towns. The firm of Godeffroy strenuously supported these proposals, and did very much to obtain for them the support of the Hanse traders and financiers. In return, the Government proposed in the Reichstag to guarantee the dividend of 4½ per cent to the new company for twenty years. Unfortunately for Herr Godeffroy he had forgotten to talk over the Reichstag, and the proposal was rejected. So, for the moment, the German Government failed to step into Samoa over the financial corpse of J. C. Godeffroy & Son by the process through which that Government between 1880 and 1890 stepped into East Africa over the financial corpse of the Deutsch-Ostafrikanische Gesellschaft, or through which the British Government stepped into East Africa and Uganda over the financial corpse of the British East Africa Company, or through which, in 1902, the French Government all but succeeded in stepping into Abyssinia over the financial corpse of the Compagnie Impériale des Chemins de Fer éthiopiens. It should, however, be remarked that the firm of J. C. Godeffroy was not as moribund as it appeared to be in 1878. It continued through its Bismarckian manager, Theodor Weber, to be "all-powerful" in Samoa, and its influence and machinations led finally to the treaties and annexations of 1899 and 1900.

The close connection between the colonial policy and commercial interests is very clear in this case of Samoa. It is no less clear in the developments which followed upon the publication of Fabri's book. A few facts will prove this. Fabri immediately became one of the leading exponents of imperialist policy. He was joined in his propaganda and schemes by the Hamburg wholesale merchant and shipper, C. Woermann. The firm of Woermann and the

Woermann Line were in process of becoming a dominating German commercial and financial interest in Africa. In 1880 Woermann joined Fabri in founding the Westdeutsche Verein für Kolonisation und Export, which started a plantation enterprise in the Cameroons, where a Woermann had already in 1868 made a commercial settlement. Fabri himself was in the 'early '80's working with von Maltzan, the founder of the Kolonialverein, which was a powerful influence in spreading imperialist and colonial ideas. The methods of this Association are admirably explained in the advice given to von Maltzan by two prominent imperialists. "Make yourself," wrote Gustav Freytag,[4] "a focus for the wishes and interests of our traders on unappropriated coast lands [of Africa] . . . undismayed by occasional failure of endeavour, . . . and I am convinced that the day will come when suddenly and unawares a German warship will produce a *fait accompli* there, where the Association shall have prepared the ground." And Prince Hohenlohe[5] in advising the establishment by the Association of "Handelsstationen" with State guarantee, wrote: "Naturally the Association must work in close harmony with the large Hamburg and Bremen firms." It would take too long to unravel and explain the complicated relations between the various propagandist Associations and commercial companies, between the literary and political imperialist agitators like Fabri, von Maltzan, and Prince Hohenlohe, the traders and financiers like Woermann of Hamburg and Lüderitz of Bremen, and the explorers like Peters and the Dernhardts. But these three groups in Germany, just as in Britain and France, were working closely together. Their policy was that described in the quotation from Freytag, and their motives were

4 Freytag: well-known German novelist, dramatist, and critic. [Editor's note]
5 Prince Hermann zu Hohenlohe-Langenburg: German soldier, politician, and president (1882) of the Kolonialverein. Not to be confused with Prince Chlodwig zu Hohenlohe-Schillingsfürst, of another branch of the family: Chancellor of Germany, 1894–1900. [Editor's note]

almost entirely economic. They aimed at starting commercial and financial enterprises in "unappropriated countries," and then at the appropriate moment, through the pressure of a public opinion which they themselves had created at home, to force the hand of the Government to send a "German warship" and thus present the world with the *fait accompli* of economic imperialism.

In 1880 Bismarck was the German equivalent of a Little Englander. By 1885 the imperialists, explorers, and traders had forced his hand and converted him ostensibly to a policy of imperialism. His policy and his imperialism were purely economic. The causes of this conversion and the facts connected with it throw great light upon the general motives of modern imperialism. First of all, let us examine the immediate influences within Germany which were brought to bear upon Bismarck. They were commercial and financial. Bismarck's change of policy was actually shown by his extending the power and rule of the German State to four places in Africa, South-West Africa, the Cameroons, Togoland, and East Africa. Now in South-West Africa the immediate impulse came from Lüderitz, the Bremen merchant, who after a year's hard work at last in 1883 obtained official backing from the Chancellor for his enterprise. And it is significant that the financial backing of the German West African Company, which took over Lüderitz's newly acquired interests in 1885, came from the financiers Hansemann and Bleichröder, to whose connection with German colonial policy we have previously had to refer. In the Cameroons the impulse came from Woermann, the Hamburg trader and ally of Fabri, who, in 1884, laid before Bismarck, at the Chancellor's request, a memorandum suggesting steps to be taken for protecting German commercial interests in the Cameroons. This memorandum formed the basis of Bismarck's instructions to the Nachtigal expedition which acquired the Cameroons for Germany. In Togoland Woermann again was chiefly responsible, for, as soon as Bismarck's consent to the occupation of South-West Africa became known, Woermann despatched an agent to prepare the way for similar action in Togoland, and in 1885 similar action followed. In East Africa the course of events was even more illuminating. In 1884 Dr. Peters the explorer arrived in Zanzibar with the intention of obtaining certain "concessions" on the coast. The German consul, acting on direct orders from Bismarck, refused him all Government protection or encouragement. He then turned to the business firms, and from them, *e.g.* Hansing & Co., he obtained every assistance. Owing to their help he succeeded in making various treaties with the natives for concessions of land. He then returned to Berlin and, now heavily backed by the commercial interests, betook himself to that same Geheimrat von Kusserow of the Foreign Office who had proved so useful to Herr Godeffroy in his financial difficulties. Peters and the German traders in East Africa found no more difficulty in talking over von Kusserow than had Herr Godeffroy in the case of Samoa. And von Kusserow once more talked over Bismarck, this time, it is said, by his glowing account of East Africa. The result was a charter for Peters' Deutsch-Ostafrikanische Gesellschaft.

Thus the immediate impulse which caused the German State to lay its hand upon islands in the Pacific, upon Togoland and the Cameroons, and South-West and East Africa, came from trade and finance, from the Godeffroys, Woermanns, Lüderitz's, and Hansings. In Germany these traders, shippers, and financiers prepared the ground by working upon public opinion through their agents, the agitators, politicians, and civil servants, like Fabri, Hohenlohe, von Maltzan, and von Kusserow; in Africa they prepared the ground by working upon the natives through their agents, the explorers, like Dr. Peters and Flegel. But the economic impulse is shown not only in these subterranean workings and interconnections: it is shown just as

clearly in the words and actions by which Bismarck expressed the new policy of the German State. For the preliminary step to Bismarck's public change of policy was his circular to the senates of the Hanse towns asking for their recommendations with respect to the difficulties and interests of firms operating in Africa. In other words, the Chancellor consulted only economic interests and thought only of economic motives. And when he had determined upon his new policy and publicly announced it, he showed that it was the policy of the flag following and protecting trade, and that the centre of it was the German trader (*der deutsche Kaufman*). "It is not possible," he said in 1884, "to conquer oversea territories by men-of-war or to take possession of them without further ceremony. Nevertheless the German trader wherever he has settled will be protected, and wherever he has assumed possession of territory there the Administration will follow him, as England has continually done." And in the Reichstag, on June 26, 1884, he made his policy and objects even more plain: "Our purpose is therefore to found not provinces but commercial enterprises: but it is also our purpose that these enterprises in their highest development shall acquire a sovereignty, a commercial sovereignty resting ultimately upon the support of the German Empire and standing under its protection, and that we shall protect them not only against the attacks of their immediate neighbours, but also against any harms or harassings which may come from other European Powers."

Practically the whole of contemporary and historical German opinion agrees that the new colonial policy of Germany in the '80's was due to economic beliefs and desires. An historian like A. Zimmermann, looking back in 1914, writes that Germany's need for colonies arose from a need for assuring to herself markets in which she could buy and sell in a world rapidly narrowing through protection and commercial competition. He agrees, therefore, with a contemporary like Fabri, who wrote in 1882 to von Maltzan: "Fiscal reforms and other similar legislation may be necessary, but all these represent only financial alterations of the national property, while our enterprises overseas have in view the increase of Germany's productive power, the raising of the national income, etc." We have seen that Bismarck had for long shown no sympathy for the current of opinion represented by Fabri, but that suddenly between 1880 and 1884 he yielded, accepted the view of economic imperialism, and reversed his policy. The wider causes of this conversion are not without importance. Bismarck was not a man to yield easily to clamour or agitation, whether of democrats, catholics, socialists, or traders and financiers. No statesman could be more unmalleable when he liked to the backstairs influences of the von Hansemanns and von Kusserows of the world, or more contemptuous of the kind of propaganda which takes the form of a National Association for establishing the millennium, abolishing poverty, or more often filling somebody's pocket. He was one of those rare statesmen who never allow an agitation to force his hand until he has himself decided to open it for a reason of his own, undreamt of by the agitators. On the face of it, it was Woermann, Lüderitz, and their open and secret agents who converted the Chancellor to economic imperialism; in reality it was another German, Leopold I. of Belgium, who combined the business of a monarch with the profession of knight-errant of Christian civilization, and the profession of a crusader with the business of an extremely shady company promoter. For the proper appreciation of the extra-European policies of the Great Powers in the last twenty years of the nineteenth century it is essential to understand the part played by Leopold in loosing modern economic imperialism into Africa.

In 1880 a conscious policy of economic imperialism hardly existed. The European traders and financiers competed on the coasts of Africa, and up and down the length of Asia, with little or no help and interference from their own Governments. The European State had not yet been impelled by economic motives and interests to penetrate either continent, and its power was nowhere used or its sovereignty extended over the inhabitants and territory of Asia or Africa in order to promote the economic interests of its European subjects. Africa was unpartitioned, and in Asia only India and a few other places were under European dominion. But certain dates and facts are significant. Between 1874 and 1877 Stanley accomplished his famous journey in Africa. In 1878 Leopold of Belgium received Stanley in Brussels. In the same year the King formed in Brussels the "Comité d'Études du Haut Congo." This was an international Committee for the purposes of science and exploration. A year later the Committee was converted into the "Association Internationale du Congo." The Association was still ostensibly international, and to the outside world seemed to have the same laudable and disinterested objects as the Committee. In reality a tremendous change had come over the Association and the objects of its royal founder. Mr. Stanley entered its service and proceeded to the Congo in 1879 to found "stations," and to make treaties with the native chiefs in the name of the Association. In 1880 the first station was established at Vivi, and in 1880 the Association became a purely Belgian enterprise. This event, acting upon desires and beliefs, ready to turn in this direction or that, was the small act, like the pressing of a button or the turning of a screw, which set in motion the terrific forces of national policies, which swung Europe into the road of Empire and the bitter rivalries of economic imperialism, which filled Asia and Africa with the explorers, the soldiers and administrators, the traders and capitalists, the missionaries, the law, order, drunkenness, religion, exploitation, and efficiency of Europe. . . .

IMPERIALISM AS A SOCIAL ATAVISM

JOSEPH A. SCHUMPETER

Born in Moravia and educated in Vienna, Joseph A. Schumpeter (1883–1950) taught economics in Austria and Germany until 1932, and in 1919–20 was Austrian Minister of Finance. He went to Harvard University in 1932 and remained there as a professor until his death. Famous in economic circles while still in his twenties, he then and later published a series of imposing economic works, among which were *The Theory of Economic Development, Business Cycles,* and *Capitalism, Socialism, and Democracy.* Schumpeter's semiconservative economic system was one of stupendous scope and in no way confined to purely economic matters, as the following extract illustrates. The essay on "imperialism" was published in German in 1919 but was not widely recognized in America until its English publication in 1951.

THE PROBLEM

No one calls it imperialism when a state, no matter how brutally and vigorously, pursues concrete interests of its own; and when it can be expected to abandon its aggressive attitude as soon as it has attained what it was after. The word "imperialism" has been abused as a slogan to the point where it threatens to lose all meaning, but up to this point our definition is quite in keeping with common usage, even in the press. For whenever the word imperialism is used, there is always the implication — whether sincere or not — of an aggressiveness, the true reasons for which do not lie in the aims which are temporarily being pursued; of an aggressiveness that is only kindled anew by each success; of an aggressiveness for its own sake, as reflected in such terms as "hegemony," "world dominion," and so forth. And history, in truth, shows us nations and classes — most nations furnish an example at some time or other — that seek expansion for the sake of expanding, war for the sake of fighting, victory for the sake of winning, dominion for the sake of ruling. This determination cannot be explained by any of the pretexts that bring it into action, by any of the aims for which it seems to be struggling at the time. It confronts us, independent of all concrete purpose or occasion, as an enduring disposition, seizing upon one opportunity as eagerly as the next. It shines through all the arguments put forward on behalf of present aims. It values conquest not so much on account of the immediate advantages — advantages that more often than not are more than dubious, or that are heedlessly cast away with the same frequency — as because it *is* conquest, success, action. Here the theory of concrete interest in our sense fails. What needs to be explained is how the will to victory itself came into being.

Expansion for its own sake always requires, among other things, concrete objects

From Joseph A. Schumpeter, *Imperialism and Social Classes,* trans. by Heinz Norden, ed. by Paul M. Sweezy (London, 1951), pp. 5–9, 12–20, 31–33, 83–96, 117–125, 128–129. By permission of the President and Fellows of Harvard College.

if it is to reach the action stage and maintain itself, but this does not constitute its meaning. Such expansion is in a sense its own "object," and the truth is that it has no adequate object beyond itself. Let us therefore, in the absence of a better term, call it "objectless." It follows for that very reason that, just as such expansion cannot be explained by concrete interest, so too it is never satisfied by the fulfillment of a concrete interest, as would be the case if fulfillment were the motive, and the struggle for it merely a necessary evil — a counterargument, in fact. Hence the tendency of such expansion to transcend all bounds and tangible limits, to the point of utter exhaustion. This, then, is our definition: imperialism is the objectless disposition on the part of a state to unlimited forcible expansion.

Now it may be possible, in the final analysis, to give an "economic explanation" for this phenomenon, to end up with economic factors. Two different points present themselves in this connection: First, an attempt can be made, following the basic idea of the economic interpretation of history, to derive imperialist tendencies from the economic-structural influences that shape life in general and from the relations of production. I should like to emphasize that I do not doubt in the least that this powerful instrument of analysis will stand up here in the same sense that it has with other, similar phenomena — if only it is kept in mind that customary modes of

political thought and feeling in a given age can never be mere "reflexes" of, or counterparts to, the production situation of that age. Because of the persistence of such habits, they will always, to a considerable degree, be dominated by the production context of past ages. Again, the attempt may be made to reduce imperialist phenomena to economic class *interests* of the age in question. This is precisely what neo-Marxist theory does. Briefly, it views imperialism simply as the reflex of the interests of the capitalist upper stratum, at a given stage of capitalist development. Beyond doubt this is by far the most serious contribution toward a solution of our problem. Certainly there is much truth in it. We shall deal with this theory later. But let us emphasize even here that it does not, of logical necessity, follow from the economic interpretation of history. It may be discarded without coming into conflict with that interpretation; indeed, without even departing from its premises. It is the treatment of this factor that constitutes the contribution of the present inquiry into the sociology of the *Zeitgeist*.

Our method of investigation is simple: we propose to analyze the birth and life of imperialism by means of historical examples which I regard as typical. A common basic trait emerges in every case, making a single sociological problem of imperialism in all ages, though there are substantial differences among the individual cases. Hence the plural, "imperialisms," in the title.

IMPERIALISM AS A CATCH PHRASE

An example will suffice. . . .

. . . The [British] election campaign of 1874 — or, to fix the date exactly, Disraeli's speech in the Crystal Palace in 1872 — marked the birth of imperialism as the catch phrase of domestic policy.

It was put in the form of "Imperial Federation." The colonies — of which Disraeli in 1852 had written: "These wretched colonies . . . are a millstone round

our necks" (Malmesbury, *Memoirs of an Ex-Minister,* p. 343) — these same colonies were to become autonomous members in a unified empire. This empire was to form a customs union. The free soil of the colonies was to remain reserved for Englishmen. A uniform defense system was to be created. The whole structure was to be crowned by a central representative organ in London, creating a closer, living connection between the imperial government and the colonies. The appeal to national sentiment, the battle cry against "Liberal" cosmopolitanism, already emerged sharply, just as they did later on in the agitation sponsored by Chamberlain, on whom fell Disraeli's mantle. Of itself the plan showed no inherent tendency to reach out beyond the "Empire," and "the Preservation of the Empire" was and is a good description of it. If we nevertheless include the "Imperial Federation" plan under the heading of imperialism, this is because its protective tariff, its militarist sentiments, its ideology of a unified "Greater Britain" all foreshadowed vague aggressive trends that would have emerged soon enough if the plan had ever passed from the sphere of the slogan into the realm of actual policy.

That it was not without value as a slogan is shown by the very fact that a man of Chamberlain's political instinct took it up — characteristically enough in another period, when effective Conservative rallying cries were at a premium. Indeed, it never vanished again, becoming a stock weapon in the political arsenal of English Conservatism, usurped even by many Liberals. As early as the nineties it meant a great deal to the youth of Oxford and Cambridge. It played a leading part in the Conservative press and at Conservative rallies. Commercial advertising grew very fond of employing its emblems — which explains why it was so conspicuous to foreign (and usually superficial) observers, and why there was so much discussion in the foreign press about "British Imperialism," a topic, moreover, that was most welcome to many political parties on the Continent. This success is readily explained. In the first place, the plan had much to offer to a whole series of special interests — primarily a protective tariff and the prospect of lucrative opportunities for exploitation, inaccessible to industry under a system of free trade. Here was the opportunity to smother consumer resistance in a flood of patriotic enthusiasm. Later on, this advantage weighed all the more heavily in the balance, for certain English industries were beginning to grow quite sensitive to the dumping tactics employed by German and American exporters. Equally important was the fact that such a plan was calculated to divert the attention of the people from social problems at home. But the main thing, before which all arguments stemming from calculating self-interest must recede into the background, was the unfailing power of the appeal to national sentiment. No other appeal is as effective, except at a time when the people happen to be caught in the midst of flaming social struggle. All other appeals are rooted in interests that must be grasped by reason. This one alone arouses the dark powers of the subconscious, calls into play instincts that carry over from the life habits of the dim past. Driven out everywhere else, the irrational seeks refuge in nationalism — the irrational which consists of belligerence, the need to hate, a goodly quota of inchoate idealism, the most naive (and hence also the most unrestrained) egotism. This is precisely what constitutes the impact of nationalism. It satisfies the need for surrender to a concrete and familiar superpersonal cause, the need for self-glorification and violent self-assertion. Whenever a vacuum arises in the mind of a people — as happens especially after exhausting social agitation, or after a war — the nationalist element comes to the fore. The idea of "Imperial Federation" gave form and direction to these trends in England. It was, in truth, a fascinating vision which was unfolded before the provincial mind. An additional factor was a vague faith in the advantages of colonial possessions, preferably to be exploited to the exclusion of all foreigners. Here we see ancient notions still at work. Once upon a time it had been feasible to treat colonies in the way that highwaymen treat their victims, and the possession of colonies unquestionably brought advantages. Trade had been possible only under immediate military protection and there could be no question that military bases were necessary. It is because of the survival of such arguments that colonialism is not yet dead, even in England today, though only in exceptional circumstances do colonies under free trade become objects of exploitation in a sense different from that in which independent countries can be exploited. And finally, there is the instinctive urge to domination. Objectively, the man in the street derives little enough satisfaction even from modern English colonial policy, but he does take pleasure in the idea, much as a card player vicariously satisfies his primitive aggressive instincts. At the time of the Boer War there was not a beggar in London who did not speak of "our" rebellious subjects. These circumstances, in all their melancholy irony, are serious factors in politics. They eliminate many courses of action that alone seem reasonable to the leaders. Here is an example: In 1815 the Ionian Islands became an English protectorate, not to be surrendered until 1863. Long before then, however, one foreign secretary after another had realized that this possession was meaningless and untenable — not in the absolute sense, but simply because no reasonable person in England would have approved of the smallest sacrifice on its behalf. Nevertheless, none dared surrender it, for it was clear that this would have appeared as a loss and a defeat, chalked up against the cabinet in question. The only thing to do was to insist that Corfu was a military base of the highest importance which must be retained. Now, during his first term as head of the government,[1] Gladstone had frequently made concessions — to Russia, to America, to others. At bottom everyone was glad that he had made them. Yet an uncomfortable feeling persisted, together with the occasion for much speech-making about national power and glory. The political genius who headed the opposition party saw all this — and *spoke* accordingly.

That this imperialism is no more than a

phrase is seen from the fact that Disraeli *spoke,* but did not *act.* But this alone is not convincing. After all, he might have lacked the opportunity to act. The crucial factor is that he *did* have the opportunity. He had a majority. He was master of his people as only an English prime minister can be. The time was auspicious. The people had lost patience with Gladstone's peace-loving nature. Disraeli owed his success in part to the slogan we have been discussing. Yet he did not even try to follow through. He took not a single step in that direction. He scarcely even mentioned it in his speeches, once it had served his purpose. His foreign policy moved wholly within the framework of Conservative tradition. For this reason it was pro-Austrian and pro-Turkish. The notion that the integrity of Turkey was in the English interest was still alive, not yet overthrown by the power of Gladstone's Midlothian speeches which were to change public opinion on this point and later, under Salisbury, invade even the Conservative credo. Hence the new Earl of Beaconsfield supported Turkey, hence he tore up the Treaty of San Stefano. Yet even this, and the capture of Cyprus, were of no avail. A tide of public indignation toppled his rule soon afterward.

We can see that Beaconsfield was quite right in not taking a single step in the direction of practical imperialism and that his policy was based on good sense. The masses of the British electorate would never have sanctioned an imperialist policy, would never have made sacrifices for it. As a toy, as a political arabesque, they accepted imperialism, just so long as no one tried it in earnest. This is seen conclusively when the fate of Chamberlain's agitation is traced. Chamberlain was unquestionably serious. A man of great talent, he rallied every ounce of personal and political power, marshaled tremendous resources, organized all the interests that stood to gain, employed a consummate propaganda technique — all this to the limits of the possible. Yet England rejected him, turning over the reins

---

[1] Between 1868 and 1885, William Gladstone, in 1868–74 and 1880–85, and Benjamin Disraeli, in 1868 and 1874–80, alternated as prime ministers of Great Britain. Disraeli was created Earl of Beaconsfield in 1876. [Editor's note]

to the opposition by an overwhelming majority.[2] It condemned the Boer War, did
everything in its power to "undo" it, proving that it was merely a chance aberration
from the general trend. So complete was
the defeat of imperialism that the Conservatives under Bonar Law, in order to
achieve some degree of political rehabilita-
tion, had to strike from their program the
tariffs on food imports, necessarily the basis
for any policy of colonial preference.

The rejection of imperialism meant the
rejection of all the interests and arguments
on which the movement was based. The
elements that were decisive for the formation of political will power — above all the
radicals and gradually the labor representatives as well — showed little enthusiasm for
the ideology of world empire. They were
much more inclined to give credence to the
Disraeli of 1852, who had compared colonies to millstones, than to the Disraeli of
1874, to the Chamberlain of the eighties
rather than the Chamberlain of 1903. They
showed not the least desire to make presents to agriculture, whether from national
or other pretexts, at the expense of the
general welfare. They were far too well
versed in the free-trade argument — and
this applies to the very lowest layers of the
English electorate — to believe the gloomy
prophecies of the "yellow press," which
insisted that free trade was sacrificing to
current consumer interests employment opportunities and the very roots of material
welfare. After all, the rise of British export trade after 1900 belied this argument
as plainly as could be. Nor had they any
sympathy for military splendor and adven-

tures in foreign policy. The whole struggle
served only to demonstrate the utter im-
potence of jingoism. The question of "objective interest" — that is, whether and to
what extent there is an economic interest
in a policy of imperialism — remains to be
discussed. Here we are concerned only
with those political notions that have
proved effective — whether they were false
or true.

What effect the present war will have
in this respect remains to be seen. For our
purposes what has still to be shown is how
this anti-imperialist sentiment — and especially anti-imperialism in practice — developed in England. In the distant past
England did have imperialist tendencies,
just as most other nations did. The process
that concerns us now begins with the moment when the struggle between the people
and the crown ended differently in England from the way it did on the Continent
— namely, with the victory of the people.
Under the Tudors and Stuarts the absolute
monarchy developed in England much as
it did at the same time on the Continent.
Specifically, the British Crown also succeeded in winning over part of the nobility,
the "cavaliers," who subsequently sided
with it against the "roundheads" and who,
but for the outcome of the battles of
Naseby and Marston Moor, would surely
have become a military palace guard. Presumably England, too, would then have
seen the rise of an arbitrary military absolutism, and the same tendencies which we
shall discover elsewhere would have led to
continual wars of aggression there too. . . .

IMPERIALISM IN PRACTICE

What imperialism looks like when it is
not mere words, and what problems it
offers, can best be illustrated by examples
from antiquity. We shall select the Egyp-

tian, Assyrian, and Persian empires and
later add certain examples from a more recent period of history. We shall find characteristic differences among them, as well
as one basic trait common to all, even the
most modern brand of imperialism — a trait

[2] In the election of 1905. [Editor's note]

which for that reason alone cannot very well be the product of modern economic evolution.

The case of Egypt, down to the Persian occupation, is particularly instructive, because here we see the imperialist trend toward expansion actually in the making. The Egyptians of the "Old" and "Middle" Empires — down to the Hyksos invasion — were a nation of peasants. The soil was the property of a hereditary, latifundian nobility which let it out to the peasants and which ruled in the political sense as well. This fundamental fact found organizational expression in a "regional" feudalism, an institution that was for the most part hereditary, rooted in real property, and, especially during the Middle Empire, quite independent of the crown. This social structure bore all the outward marks of force, yet it lacked any inherent tendency toward violent and unlimited expansion. The external situation ruled out such a trend; for the country, while easy to defend, was quite unsuitable as a base for a policy of conquest in the grand manner. Nor was it demanded by economic requirements — and indeed, no trace of such a policy is apparent. Throughout the period of the "Old" Empire of Memphis we learn of but one warlike undertaking (except for unimportant fighting on the Sinai peninsula). This was the campaigns in southern Syria under the Sixth Dynasty. In the "Middle" Empire of Thebes things were not quite so peaceful; still, fighting revolved essentially only about the defense of the frontiers. The single conquest was Nubia (under Amenemhat I and Usertesen III).

Things changed only after the expulsion of the Hyksos (whom Manetho counts as the Fifteenth and Sixteenth Dynasties), in the "New" Empire. The immediate successors of the liberator, Aahmes I, already conquered upper Cush to the third cataract and then reached farther into Asia. They grew more and more aggressive, and campaign followed campaign, without the slightest concrete cause. Dhutmes III and Amenhotep III were conquerors, pure and

simple. In the end Egyptian rule reached to the Amanes and beyond the Euphrates. Following a reversal under the Nineteenth and Twentieth Dynasties, this policy was resumed, and after the Assyrian invasion (662) and the liberation by Psamtik I, Egypt, reunited under Necho II, again passed over to the attack, until the Battle of Karkamish (604) put an end to its Asiatic undertakings. Why did all this happen?

The facts enable us to diagnose the case. The war of liberation from the Hyksos, lasting a century and a half, had "militarized" Egypt. A class of professional soldiers had come into being, replacing the old peasant militia and technically far superior to it, owing to the employment of battle chariots, introduced, like the horse, by the Bedouin Hyksos. The support of that class enabled the victorious kings, as early as Aahmes I, to reorganize the empire centrally and to suppress the regional feudal lords and the large, aristocratic landowners — or at least to reduce their importance. We hear little about them in the "New" Empire. The crown thus carried out a social revolution; it became the ruling power, together with the new military and hierarchical aristocracy and, to an increasing degree, foreign mercenaries as well. This new social and political organization was essentially a war machine. It was motivated by warlike instincts and interests. Only in war could it find an outlet and maintain its domestic position. Without continual passages at arms it would necessarily have collapsed. Its external orientation was war, and war alone. Thus war became the normal condition, alone conducive to the well-being of the organs of the body social that now existed. To take the field was a matter of course, the reasons for doing so were of subordinate importance. *Created by wars that required it, the machine now created the wars it required.* A will for broad conquest without tangible limits, for the capture of positions that were manifestly untenable — this was typical imperialism. . . .

IMPERIALISM AND CAPITALISM

Our analysis of the historical evidence has shown, first, the unquestionable fact that "objectless" tendencies toward forcible expansion, without definite, utilitarian limits — that is, non-rational and irrational, purely instinctual inclinations toward war and conquest — play a very large role in the history of mankind. It may sound paradoxical, but numberless wars — perhaps the majority of all wars — have been waged without adequate "reason" — not so much from the moral viewpoint as from that of reasoned and reasonable interest. The most herculean efforts of the nations, in other words, have faded into the empty air. Our analysis, in the second place, provides an explanation for this drive to action, this will to war — a theory by no means exhausted by mere references to an "urge" or an "instinct." The explanation lies, instead, in the vital needs of situations that molded peoples and classes into warriors — if they wanted to avoid extinction — and in the fact that psychological dispositions and social structures acquired in the dim past in such situations, once firmly established, tend to maintain themselves and to continue in effect long after they have lost their meaning and their life-preserving function. Our analysis, in the third place, has shown the existence of subsidiary factors that facilitate the survival of such dispositions and structures — factors that may be divided into two groups. The orientation toward war is mainly fostered by the domestic interests of ruling classes, but also by the influence of all those who stand to gain individually from a war policy, whether economically or socially. Both groups of factors are generally overgrown by elements of an altogether different character, not only in terms of political phraseology, but also of psychological motivation. Imperialisms differ greatly in detail, but they all have at least these traits in common, turning them into a single phenomenon in the field of sociology, as we noted in the introduction.

Imperialism thus is atavistic in character. It falls into that large group of surviving features from earlier ages that play such an important part in every concrete social situation. In other words, it is an element that stems from the living conditions, not of the present, but of the past — or, put in terms of the economic interpretation of history, from past rather than present relations of production. It is an atavism in the social structure, in individual, psychological habits of emotional reaction. Since the vital needs that created it have passed away for good, it too must gradually disappear, even though every warlike involvement, no matter how non-imperialist in character, tends to revive it. It tends to disappear as a structural element because the structure that brought it to the fore goes into a decline, giving way, in the course of social development, to other structures that have no room for it and eliminate the power factors that supported it. It tends to disappear as an element of habitual emotional reaction, because of the progressive rationalization of life and mind, a process in which old functional needs are absorbed by new tasks, in which heretofore military energies are functionally modified. If our theory is correct, cases of imperialism should decline in intensity the later they occur in the history of a people and of a culture. Our most recent examples of unmistakable, clear-cut imperialism are the absolute monarchies of the eighteenth century. They are unmistakably "more civilized" than their predecessors.

It is from absolute autocracy that the present age has taken over what imperialist tendencies it displays. And the imperialism of absolute autocracy flourished before the Industrial Revolution that created the modern world, or rather, before the consequences of that revolution began to be felt in all their aspects. These two statements are primarily meant in a historical sense, and as such they are no more than self-evident. We shall nevertheless try, within the framework of our theory, to define the significance of capitalism for our phenomenon and to examine the relationship between present-day imperialist tendencies and the autocratic imperialism of the eighteenth century.

The floodtide that burst the dams in the Industrial Revolution had its sources, of course, back in the Middle Ages. But capitalism began to shape society and impress its stamp on every page of social history only with the second half of the eighteenth century. Before that time there had been only islands of capitalist economy imbedded in an ocean of village and urban economy. True, certain political influences emanated from these islands, but they were able to assert themselves only indirectly. Not until the process we term the Industrial Revolution did the working masses, led by the entrepreneur, overcome the bonds of older life-forms — the environment of peasantry, guild, and aristocracy. The causal connection was this: A transformation in the basic economic factors (which need not detain us here) created the objective opportunity for the production of commodities, for large-scale industry, working for a market of customers whose individual identities were unknown, operating solely with a view to maximum financial profit. It was this opportunity that created an economically oriented leadership — personalities whose field of achievement was the organization of such commodity production in the form of capitalist enterprise. Successful enterprises in large numbers represented something new in the economic and social sense. They fought for and won freedom of action. They compelled state policy to adapt itself to their needs. More and more they attracted the most vigorous leaders from other spheres, as well as the manpower of those spheres, causing them and the social strata they represented to languish. Capitalist entrepreneurs fought the former ruling circles for a share in state control, for leadership in the state. The very fact of their success, their position, their resources, their power, raised them in the political and social scale. Their

mode of life, their cast of mind became increasingly important elements on the social scene. Their actions, desires, needs, and beliefs emerged more and more sharply within the total picture of the social community. In a historical sense, this applied primarily to the industrial and financial leaders of the movement — the bourgeoisie. But soon it applied also to the working masses which this movement created and placed in an altogether new class situation. This situation was governed by new forms of the working day, of family life, of interests — and these, in turn, corresponded to new orientations toward the social structure as a whole. More and more, in the course of the nineteenth century, the typical modern worker came to determine the overall aspect of society; for competitive capitalism, by its inherent logic, kept on raising the demand for labor and thus the economic level and social power of the workers, until this class too was able to assert itself in a political sense. The working class and its mode of life provided the type from which the intellectual developed. Capitalism did not create the intellectuals — the "new middle class." But in earlier times only the legal scholar, the cleric, and the physician had formed a special intellectual class, and even they had enjoyed but little scope for playing an independent role. Such opportunities were provided only by capitalist society, which created the industrial and financial bureaucrat, the journalist, and so on, and which opened up new vistas to the jurist and physician. The "professional" of capitalist society arose as a class type. Finally, as a class type, the rentier, the beneficiary of industrial loan capital, is also a creature of capitalism. All these types are shaped by the capitalist mode of production, and they tend for this reason to bring other types — even the peasant — into conformity with themselves.

These new types were now cast adrift from the fixed order of earlier times, from the environment that had shackled and protected people for centuries, from the old associations of village, manor house, clan fellowship, often even from families in the broader sense. They were severed from the things that had been constant year after year, from cradle to grave — tools, homes, the countryside, especially the soil. They were on their own, enmeshed in the pitiless logic of gainful employment, mere drops in the vast ocean of industrial life, exposed to the inexorable pressures of competition. They were freed from the control of ancient patterns of thought, of the grip of institutions and organs that taught and represented these outlooks in village, manor, and guild. They were removed from the old world, engaged in building a new one for themselves — a specialized, mechanized world. Thus they were all inevitably democratized, individualized, and rationalized. They were democratized, because the picture of time-honored power and privilege gave way to one of continual change, set in motion by industrial life. They were individualized, because subjective opportunities to shape their lives took the place of immutable objective factors. They were rationalized, because the instability of economic position made their survival hinge on continual, deliberately rationalistic decisions — a dependence that emerged with great sharpness. Trained to economic rationalism, these people left no sphere of life unrationalized, questioning everything about themselves, the social structure, the state, the ruling class. The marks of this process are engraved on every aspect of modern culture. It is this process that explains the basic features of that culture.

These are things that are well known today, recognized in their full significance — indeed, often exaggerated. Their application to our subject is plain. Everything that is purely instinctual, everything insofar as it is purely instinctual, is driven into the background by this development. It creates a social and psychological atmosphere in keeping with modern economic forms, where traditional habits, merely because they were traditional, could no more survive than obsolete economic forms. Just as the latter can survive only if they are

continually "adapted," so instinctual tendencies can survive only when the conditions that gave rise to them continue to apply, or when the "instinct" in question derives a new purpose from new conditions. The "instinct" that is *only* "instinct," that has lost its purpose, languishes relatively quickly in the capitalist world, just as does an inefficient economic practice. We see this process of rationalization at work even in the case of the strongest impulses. We observe it, for example, in the facts of procreation. We must therefore anticipate finding it in the case of the imperialist impulse as well; we must expect to see this impulse, which rests on the primitive contingencies of physical combat, gradually disappear, washed away by new exigencies of daily life. There is another factor too. The competitive system absorbs the full energies of most of the people at all economic levels. Constant application, attention, and concentration of energy are the conditions of survival within it, primarily in the specifically economic professions, but also in other activities organized on their model. There is much less excess energy to be vented in war and conquest than in any precapitalist society. What excess energy there is flows largely into industry itself, accounts for its shining figures — the type of the captain of industry — and for the rest is applied to art, science, and the social struggle. In a purely capitalist world, what was once energy for war becomes simply energy for labor of every kind. Wars of conquest and adventurism in foreign policy in general are bound to be regarded as troublesome distractions, destructive of life's meaning, a diversion from the accustomed and therefore "true" task.

A purely capitalist world therefore can offer no fertile soil to imperialist impulses. That does not mean that it cannot still maintain an interest in imperialist expansion. We shall discuss this immediately. The point is that its people are likely to be essentially of an unwarlike disposition. Hence we must expect that anti-imperialist tendencies will show themselves wherever capitalism penetrates the economy and, through the economy, the mind of modern nations — most strongly, of course, where capitalism itself is strongest, where it has advanced furthest, encountered the least resistance, and preeminently where its types and hence democracy — in the "bourgeois" sense — come closest to political dominion. We must further expect that the types formed by capitalism will actually be the carriers of these tendencies. Is such the case? The facts that follow are cited to show that this expectation, which flows from our theory, is in fact justified.

1. Throughout the world of capitalism, and specifically among the elements formed by capitalism in modern social life, there has arisen a fundamental opposition to war, expansion, cabinet diplomacy, armaments, and socially entrenched professional armies. This opposition had its origin in the country that first turned capitalist — England — and arose coincidentally with that country's capitalist development. "Philosophical radicalism" was the first politically influential intellectual movement to represent this trend successfully, linking it up, as was to be expected, with economic freedom in general and free trade in particular. Molesworth became a cabinet member, even though he had publicly declared — on the occasion of the Canadian revolution — that he prayed for the defeat of his country's arms. In step with the advance of capitalism, the movement also gained adherents elsewhere — though at first only adherents without influence. It found support in Paris — indeed, in a circle oriented toward capitalist enterprise (for example, Frédéric Passy). True, pacifism as a matter of principle had existed before, though only among a few small religious sects. But modern pacifism, in its political foundations if not its derivation, is unquestionably a phenomenon of the capitalist world.

2. Wherever capitalism penetrated, peace parties of such strength arose that virtually every war meant a political struggle on the domestic scene. The exceptions are rare —

Germany in the Franco-Prussian war of 1870–1871, both belligerents in the Russo-Turkish war of 1877–1878. That is why every war is carefully justified as a defensive war by the governments involved, and by all the political parties, in their official utterances — indicating a realization that a war of a different nature would scarcely be tenable in a political sense. (Here too the Russo-Turkish war is an exception, but a significant one.) In former times this would not have been necessary. Reference to an interest or pretense at moral justification was customary as early as the eighteenth century, but only in the nineteenth century did the assertion of attack, or the threat of attack, become the only avowed occasion for war. In the distant past, imperialism had needed no disguise whatever, and in the absolute autocracies only a very transparent one; but today imperialism is carefully hidden from public view — even though there may still be an unofficial appeal to warlike instincts. No people and no ruling class today can openly afford to regard war as a normal state of affairs or a normal element in the life of nations. No one doubts that today it must be characterized as an abnormality and a disaster. True, war is still glorified. But glorification in the style of King Tuglâtî-palisharra is rare and unleashes such a storm of indignation that every practical politician carefully dissociates himself from such things. Everywhere there is official acknowledgment that peace is an end in itself — though not necessarily an end overshadowing all purposes that can be realized by means of war. Every expansionist urge must be carefully related to a concrete goal. All this is primarily a matter of political phraseology, to be sure. But the necessity for this phraseology is a symptom of the popular attitude. And that attitude makes a policy of imperialism more and more difficult — indeed, the very word imperialism is applied only to the enemy, in a reproachful sense, being carefully avoided with reference to the speaker's own policies.

3. The type of industrial worker created

by capitalism is always vigorously anti-imperialist. In the individual case, skillful agitation may persuade the working masses to approve or remain neutral — a concrete goal or interest in self-defense always playing the main part — but no initiative for a forcible policy of expansion ever emanates from this quarter. On this point official socialism unquestionably formulates not merely the interests but also the conscious will of the workers. Even less than peasant imperialism is there any such thing as socialist or other working-class imperialism.

4. Despite manifest resistance on the part of powerful elements, the capitalist age has seen the development of methods for preventing war, for the peaceful settlement of disputes among states. The very fact of resistance means that the trend can be explained only from the mentality of capitalism as a mode of life. It definitely limits the opportunities imperialism needs if it is to be a powerful force. True, the methods in question often fail, but even more often they are successful. I am thinking not merely of the Hague Court of Arbitration but of the practice of submitting controversial issues to conferences of the major powers or at least those powers directly concerned — a course of action that has become less and less avoidable. True, here too the individual case may become a farce. But the serious setbacks of today must not blind us to the real importance or sociological significance of these things.

5. Among all capitalist economies, that of the United States is least burdened with precapitalist elements, survivals, reminiscences, and power factors. Certainly we cannot expect to find imperialist tendencies altogether lacking even in the United States, for the immigrants came from Europe with their convictions fully formed, and the environment certainly favored the revival of instincts of pugnacity. But we can conjecture that among all countries the United States is likely to exhibit the weakest imperialist trend. This turns out to be the truth. The case is particularly instructive, because the United States has seen a

particularly strong emergence of capitalist interests in an imperialist direction — those very interests to which the phenomenon of imperialism has so often been reduced, a subject we shall yet touch on. Nevertheless the United States was the first advocate of disarmament and arbitration. It was the first to conclude treaties concerning arms limitations (1817) and arbitral courts (first attempt in 1797) — doing so most zealously, by the way, when economic interest in expansion was at its greatest. Since 1908 such treaties have been concluded with twenty-two states. In the course of the nineteenth century, the United States had numerous occasions for war, including instances that were well calculated to test its patience. It made almost no use of such occasions. Leading industrial and financial circles in the United States had and still have an evident interest in incorporating Mexico into the Union. There was more than enough opportunity for such annexation — but Mexico remained unconquered. Racial catch phrases and working-class interests pointed to Japan as a possible danger. Hence possession of the Philippines was not a matter of indifference — yet surrender of this possession is being discussed. Canada was an almost defenseless prize — but Canada remained independent. Even in the United States, of course, politicians need slogans — especially slogans calculated to divert attention from domestic issues. Theodore Roosevelt and certain magnates of the press actually resorted to imperialism — and the result, in that world of high capitalism, was utter defeat, a defeat that would have been even more abject, if other slogans, notably those appealing to anti-trust sentiment, had not met with better success.

These facts are scarcely in dispute. And since they fit into the picture of the mode of life which we have recognized to be the necessary product of capitalism, since we can grasp them adequately from the necessities of that mode of life and industry, it follows that capitalism is by nature anti-imperialist. Hence we cannot readily derive from it such imperialist tendencies as actually exist, but must evidently see them only as alien elements, carried into the world of capitalism from the outside, supported by non-capitalist factors in modern life. The survival of interest in a policy of forcible expansion does not, by itself, alter these facts — not even, it must be steadily emphasized, from the viewpoint of the economic interpretation of history. . . .

* * *

. . . The character of capitalism leads to large-scale production, but with few exceptions large-scale production does *not* lead to the kind of unlimited concentration that would leave but one or only a few firms in each industry. On the contrary, any plant runs up against limits to its growth in a given location; and the growth of combinations which would make sense under a system of free trade encounters limits of organizational efficiency. Beyond these limits there is no tendency toward combination inherent in the competitive system. In particular, the rise of trusts and cartels — a phenomenon quite different from the trend to large-scale production with which it is often confused — can never be explained by the automatism of the competitive system. This follows from the very fact that trusts and cartels can attain their primary purpose — to pursue a monopoly policy — only behind protective tariffs, without which they would lose their essential significance. But protective tariffs do not automatically grow from the competitive system. They are the fruit of political action — *a type of action that by no means reflects the objective interests of all those concerned* but that, on the contrary, becomes impossible as soon as the majority of those whose consent is necessary realize their true interests. To some extent it is obvious, and for the rest it will be presently shown, that the interests of the minority, quite appropriately expressed in support of a protective tariff, do not stem from capitalism as such. It follows that *it is a basic fallacy to describe imperialism as a necessary phase of capitalism, or even to speak of the development of capitalism into imperialism.* We have seen before that the mode of life of the capitalist world does not favor imperialist attitudes. We now see that the alignment of interests in a capitalist economy — even the interests of its upper strata — by no means points unequivocally in the direction of imperialism. We now come to the final step in our line of reasoning.

Since we cannot derive even export monopolism from any tendencies of the competitive system toward big enterprise, we must find some other explanation. A glance at the original purpose of tariffs provides what we need. Tariffs sprang from the financial interests of the monarchy. They were a method of exploiting the trader which differed from the method of the robber baron in the same way that the royal chase differed from the method of the poacher. They were in line with the royal prerogatives of safe conduct, of protection for the Jews, of the granting of market rights, and so forth. From the thirteenth century onward this method was progressively refined in the autocratic state, less and less emphasis being placed on the direct monetary yield of customs revenues, and more and more on their indirect effect in creating productive taxable objects. In other words, while the protective value of a tariff counted, it counted only from the viewpoint of the ultimate monetary advantage of the sovereign. It does not matter, for our purposes, that occasionally this policy, under the influence of lay notions of economics, blundered badly in the choice of its methods. (From the viewpoint of autocratic interest, incidentally, such measures were not nearly so self-defeating as they were from the viewpoint of the national economy.) Every customs house, every privilege conferring the right to produce, market, or store, thus created a new economic situation which deflected trade and industry into "unnatural" channels. All tariffs, rights, and the like became the seed bed for economic growth that could have neither sprung up nor maintained itself without them. Further, all such economic institutions dictated by autocratic interest were surrounded by manifold interests of people who were dependent on them and now began to demand their continuance — a wholly paradoxical though at the same time quite understandable situation. The trading and manufacturing bourgeoisie was all the more aware of its dependence on the sovereign, since it needed his protection against the remaining feudal powers; and the uncertainties of the times, together with the lack of great consuming centers, impeded the rise of free economic competition. Insofar as commerce and manufacturing came into being at all, therefore, they arose under the sign of monopolistic interest. Thus the bourgeoisie willingly allowed itself to be molded into one of the power instruments of the monarchy, both in a territorial and in a national sense. It is even true that the bourgeoisie, because of the character of its interests and the kind of economic outlook that corresponded to those interests, made an essential contribution to the emergence of modern nationalism. Another factor that worked in the same direction was the financial relation between the great merchant houses and the sovereign. This theory of the nature of the relationship between the autocratic state and the bourgeoisie is not refuted by pointing out that it was precisely the mercantile republics of the Middle Ages and the early modern period that initially pursued a policy of mercantilism. They were no more than enclaves in a world pervaded by the struggle among feudal powers. The Hanseatic League and Venice, for example, could maintain themselves only as military powers, could pursue their business only by means of fortified bases, warehousing privileges, protective treaties. This forced the people to stand shoulder to shoulder, made the exploitation of political gains more important than domestic competition, infused them with a corporate and monopolistic spirit. Wherever autocratic power vanished at an early date — as in the Netherlands and later in

England — and the protective interest receded into the background, they swiftly discovered that trade must be free — "free to the nethermost recesses of hell."

Trade and industry of the early capitalist period thus remained strongly pervaded with precapitalist methods, bore the stamp of autocracy, and served its interests, either willingly or by force. With its traditional habits of feeling, thinking, and acting molded along such lines, the bourgeoisie entered the Industrial Revolution. It was shaped, in other words, by the needs and interests of an environment that was essentially non-capitalist, or at least precapitalist — needs stemming not from the nature of the capitalist economy as such but from the fact of the coexistence of early capitalism with another and at first overwhelmingly powerful mode of life and business. Established habits of thought and action tend to persist, and hence the spirit of guild and monopoly at first maintained itself, and was only slowly undermined, even where capitalism was in sole possession of the field. Actually capitalism did not fully prevail *anywhere* on the Continent. Existing economic interests, "artificially" shaped by the autocratic state, remained dependent on the "protection" of the state. The industrial organism, such as it was, would not have been able to withstand free competition. Even where the old barriers crumbled in the autocratic state, the people did not all at once flock to the clear track. They were creatures of mercantilism and even earlier periods, and many of them huddled together and protested against the affront of being forced to depend on their own ability. They cried for paternalism, for protection, for forcible restraint of strangers, and above all for tariffs. They met with partial success, particularly because capitalism failed to take radical action in the agrarian field. Capitalism did bring about many changes on the land, springing in part from its automatic mechanisms, in part from the political trends it engendered — abolition of serfdom, freeing the soil from feudal entanglements, and so on — but initially it did not alter the basic outlines of the social structure of the countryside. Even less did it affect the spirit of the people, and least of all their political goals. This explains why the features and trends of autocracy — including imperialism — proved so resistant, why they exerted such a powerful influence on capitalist development, why the old export monopolism could live on and merge into the new.

These are facts of fundamental significance to an understanding of the soul of modern Europe. Had the ruling class of the Middle Ages — the war-oriented nobility — changed its profession and function and become the ruling class of the capitalist world; or had developing capitalism swept it away, put it out of business, instead of merely clashing head-on with it in the agrarian sphere — then much would have been different in the life of modern peoples. But as things actually were, neither eventuality occurred; or, more correctly, both are taking place, only at a very slow pace. The two groups of landowners remain social classes clearly distinguishable from the groupings of the capitalist world. The social pyramid of the present age has been formed, not by the substance and laws of capitalism alone, but by two different social substances, and by the laws of two different epochs. Whoever seeks to understand Europe must not forget this and concentrate all attention on the indubitably basic truth that one of these substances tends to be absorbed by the other and thus the sharpest of all class conflicts tends to be eliminated. Whoever seeks to understand Europe must not overlook that even today its life, its ideology, its politics are greatly under the influence of the feudal "substance," that while the bourgeoisie can assert its interests everywhere, it "rules" only in exceptional circumstances, and then only briefly. The bourgeois outside his office and the professional man of capitalism outside his profession cut a very sorry figure. Their spiritual leader is the rootless "intellectual," a slender reed open to every impulse and a prey to unrestrained emo-

tionalism. The "feudal" elements, on the other hand, have both feet on the ground, even psychologically speaking. Their ideology is as stable as their mode of life. They believe certain things to be really true, others to be really false. This quality of possessing a definite character and cast of mind as a class, this simplicity and solidity of social and spiritual position extends their power far beyond their actual bases, gives them the ability to assimilate new elements, to make others serve their purposes — in a word, gives them *prestige*, something to which the bourgeois, as is well known, always looks up, something with which he tends to ally himself, despite all actual conflicts.

The nobility entered the modern world in the form into which it had been shaped by the autocratic state — the same state that had also molded the bourgeoisie. It was the sovereign who disciplined the nobility, instilled loyalty into it, "statized" it, and, as we have shown, imperialized it. He turned its nationalist sentiments — as in the case of the bourgeoisie — into an aggressive nationalism, and then made it a pillar of his organization, particularly his war machine. It had not been that in the immediately preceding period. Rising absolutism had at first availed itself of much more dependent organs. For that very reason, in his position as leader of the feudal powers and as warlord, the sovereign survived the onset of the Industrial Revolution, and as a rule — except in France — won victory over political revolution. The bourgeoisie did not simply supplant the sovereign, nor did it make him its leader, as did the nobility. It merely wrested a portion of his power from him and for the rest submitted to him. It did not take over from the sovereign the state as an abstract form of organization. The state remained a special social power, confronting the bourgeoisie. In some countries it has continued to play that role to the present day. It is in the *state* that the bourgeoisie with its interests seeks refuge, protection against external and even domestic enemies. The bourgeoisie seeks to win over the state for itself, and in return serves the state and state interests that are different from its own. Imbued with the spirit of the old autocracy, trained by it, the bourgeoisie often takes over its ideology, even where, as in France, the sovereign is eliminated and the official power of the nobility has been broken. Because the sovereign needed soldiers, the modern bourgeois—at least in his slogans—is an even more vehement advocate of an increasing population. Because the sovereign was in a position to exploit conquests, needed them to be a victorious warlord, the bourgeoisie thirsts for national glory—even in France, worshiping a headless body, as it were. Because the sovereign found a large gold hoard useful, the bourgeoisie even today cannot be swerved from its bullionist prejudices. Because the autocratic state paid attention to the trader and manufacturer chiefly as the most important sources of taxes and credits, today even the intellectual who has not a shred of property looks on international commerce, not from the viewpoint of the consumer, but from that of the trader and exporter. Because pugnacious sovereigns stood in constant fear of attack by their equally pugnacious neighbors, the modern bourgeois attributes aggressive designs to neighboring peoples. All such modes of thought are essentially noncapitalist. Indeed, they vanish most quickly wherever capitalism fully prevails. They are survivals of the autocratic alignment of interests, and they endure wherever the autocratic state endures on the old basis and with the old orientation, even though more and more democratized and otherwise transformed. They bear witness to the extent to which essentially imperialist absolutism has patterned not only the economy of the bourgeoisie but also its mind—in the interests of autocracy and against those of the bourgeoisie itself. . . .

Here we find that we have penetrated to the historical as well as the sociological sources of modern imperialism. It does not *coincide* with nationalism and militarism, though it *fuses* with them by supporting them as it is supported by them. It too is—not only historically, but also sociologically—a heritage of the autocratic state, of its structural elements, organizational forms, interest alignments, and human attitudes, the outcome of precapitalist forces which the autocratic state has reorganized, in part by the methods of early capitalism. It would never have been evolved by the "inner logic" of capitalism itself. This is true even of mere export monopolism. It too has its sources in absolutist policy and the action habits of an essentially precapitalist environment. That it was able to develop to its present dimensions is owing to the momentum of a situation once created, which continued to engender ever new "artificial" economic structures, that is, those which maintain themselves by political power alone. In most of the countries addicted to export monopolism it is also owing to the fact that the old autocratic state and the old attitude of the bourgeoisie toward it were so vigorously maintained. But export monopolism, to go a step further, is not yet imperialism. And even if it had been able to arise without protective tariffs, it would never have developed into imperialism in the hands of an unwarlike bourgeoisie. If this did happen, it was only because the heritage included the war machine, together with its socio-psychological aura and aggressive bent, and because a class oriented toward war maintained itself in a ruling position. This class clung to its domestic interest in war, and the promilitary interests among the bourgeoisie were able to ally themselves with it. This alliance kept alive war instincts and ideas of overlordship, male supremacy, and triumphant glory—ideas that would have otherwise long since died. It led to social conditions that, while they ultimately stem from the conditions of production, cannot be explained from capitalist production methods alone. And it often impresses its mark on present-day politics, threatening Europe with the constant danger of war. . . .

SCHUMPETER'S IMPERIALISM —
A CRITICAL NOTE

MURRAY GREENE

Murray Greene wrote the following essay in response to a generally favorable review of Schumpeter which appeared in an earlier issue of *Social Research*. Here Greene attacks the position of Schumpeter with careful analysis and apparently devastating precision. He also contrasts the weaknesses he finds in Schumpeter with the very ideas that Schumpeter had set out to destroy. The similarities and differences of the two interpretations are thus brought clearly into focus.

DESPITE its many brilliant individual insights, its sweeping historical range, and its bold and challenging syntheses, Schumpeter's thesis in his essay on "The Sociology of Imperialisms" is, to my mind, basically inadequate and misleading as a generalized theory of imperialism. It appears to me that the main burden of Schumpeter's argument is to show that capitalism is essentially anti-imperialist. To do this he develops a very specialized definition of imperialism which he then expounds with references to certain selected societies in history. He also sets up a very specialized definition of capitalism, which he then shows to be inconsistent with his definition of imperialism, thereby "proving" that capitalism is anti-imperialist.

I

Schumpeter defines imperialism as "the objectless disposition on the part of a state to unlimited forcible expansion." This disposition derives from a warrior-class social structure which requires "expansion for the sake of expanding, war for the sake of fighting, victory for the sake of winning, dominion for the sake of ruling."

One is immediately struck by how much is excluded by this definition. All instances in history or prehistory of expansion for the purpose of obtaining fertile land, grazing areas, hunting grounds, precious minerals, plunder, tribute, slaves, colonization areas, or commercial advantages are automatically excluded, because there was a specific object in mind. Also excluded, and most important of all for modern times, is expansion for the purpose of acquiring industrial raw materials, markets, capital investment areas, and cheap labor power. Because such instances of expansion serve a concrete interest they are not instances of imperialism. It is immediately apparent that Schumpeter's definition focuses attention exclusively on the internal compulsions of the particular expanding society, with no regard whatever for what it is that constitutes the object or goal, as such, of the expansion.

The onesidedness of Schumpeter's definition can perhaps best be shown by a comparison with the Marxist concept of capitalist imperialism. The Marxist concept also stresses the internal compulsions of the expanding society; and to a certain extent there is a similarity to the Schumpeter idea of limitlessness, in that capitalist expansion

From Murray Greene, "Schumpeter's Imperialism — A Critical Note," *Social Research. An International Quarterly of Political and Social Science*, XIX (December, 1952), 453–463. By permission of the Graduate Faculty of Political and Social Science of the New School for Social Research.

must press on and on, ever exhausting new areas of exploitation. But in the Marxist concept the relationship between subject and object is not meaningless. The subject has the need for expansion, but it is not just expansion for its own sake. The object of the expansion — markets, for example — is organically (dialectically) related to the specific needs of the subject. The expansion may be limitless, but it is not, like Schumpeter's, objectless, nor is it merely functional in a purely subjective sense.

Schumpeter's sole preoccupation with the subject is an abstraction of a portion of reality, and consequently a misleading distortion. Thus his almost ludicrous explaining away of British imperialism is not just a case of a particular miss which lowers an otherwise good batting average. It is a consequence of his subjectivistic approach, which necessarily excludes British overseas expansion — whether of the eighteenth-century period of commercial capitalism or the nineteenth-century period of industrial and finance capitalism — because in neither period could English society be termed a society based on a warrior-class social structure.

Schumpeter's additional qualification — that imperialism must be forcible — limits the definition even more. There are different kinds of force which states have applied and do apply against one another for the purpose of expansion. But Schumpeter means by force only military force. He must mean this to support his thesis. Thus one country's control of another through the superiority of its economic power (perhaps best illustrated in Latin America); the penetration of industrial products into native village or craft economies, and the shattering effects that this has on the economic and social structures of those economies (North Africa, the Near East, the Far East); the bribery or coercion of feudal chieftains or tribal leaders in an effort to persuade them to relinquish control of the labor power or resources of their domains (the Near East); the swindling of unsophisticated natives into bartering away

their land and resources for trinkets, badges of prestige, or paper treaties (Africa); the forcing of loans on spendthrift or inexperienced governments, to serve as an entering wedge for foreign control (North Africa, the Caribbean) — these and other devious means cannot, by Schumpeter's definition, be termed imperialistic.

Even the threat of force — and more often than force itself this is all that is necessary — cannot be termed imperialistic, because, for Schumpeter, it is only in the actual application of military force that imperialism serves its true function for the subject. Thus even Roman imperialism (of which Schumpeter's brief analysis is marvelously stimulating) does not properly fit into his definition, for here the imperialistic actions, designed to strengthen the latifundian landlords' control of the state apparatus and to head off internal land reform, have not the same function as those in his classic instances of the Egyptian, Assyrian, Persian, and Arab Moslem warrior societies.

Is it not strange that the two imperialisms most important for Western civilization are, in the one case, excluded altogether, and, in the other, assigned an atypical, special role — and this in a theory that purports to be a generalized definition of imperialism? Why, then, does Schumpeter construct his definition in this way? Why must imperialism be "objectless" as well as "forcible"?

The answer is that Schumpeter's imperialism is a onesided, sociological phenomenon — the expression of a warrior-class social structure which fights because it is geared to fighting and has no other reason for existence. It is obvious that if expansion had a specific, limited aim, or if it were non-forcible, it would not necessarily fit this type of society. It could, for example, be an economic phenomenon and serve a non-warrior-class structure. Thus when Schumpeter comes to the analysis of capitalism he need only apply the following syllogism, inherent in his previous build-up: what is not the expression of a warrior-class social structure is not imperialism;

capitalist society is not a warrior-class social structure; therefore capitalist society is non-imperialist. He then adds, to explain a few odds and ends, that what may look like capitalist imperialism just happens to occur in the era of capitalism, and is really only the remnants left from a past or passing age.

II

Let us now turn to Schumpeter's discussion of capitalism. Just as he abstracts from history a certain type of expansionism and terms it the true prototype of imperialism, so, too, he abstracts a certain type of capitalism and presents it as the true model of all capitalism.

Schumpeter takes the position that in capitalism there is no inherent economic drive toward imperialism. Tendencies toward economic expansionism he treats as coming under the heading of protectionism and monopolism. Protectionism and monopolism, he argues, are not endemic to capitalism, but are against its true spirit. They are opposed to the interests of most producers and of all consumers within the national economy itself, and are contrary to the interests of all nations as members of the international community. Where protectionism and monopolism exist, they are the outcome of the incomplete success of capitalism in its struggles with the monarchical power. To illustrate this, Schumpeter contrasts the early and complete success of British capitalism — and its consequent lack of tariffs and monopolies — with the partial and later development of capitalism on the Continent — and its consequent dependence on the state apparatus, which entailed carrying over ideas and practices from a former age.

As with Schumpeter's other ideas, there is some truth here; but, as elsewhere, the partial truth is used in place of the broader truth, not to supplement it. True, British capitalism of the latter half of the nineteenth century was featured by free trade. But was this because the British ruling classes were successful in their seventeenth-century struggle against the crown, or was

it because the successful outcome of that struggle resulted in conditions that paved the way for British capitalism's initial industrial supremacy and its preeminence in the markets of the world? Of course the seventeenth-century political developments were important! But can anyone possibly maintain that British capitalism of the latter half of the nineteenth century would have been what it was if, instead of having had the field to itself in the early nineteenth century, it had been confronted from the very beginning by two such rivals as Germany and the United States? Or if, from the very beginning, it had started out as Germany did — having no worldwide empire, with almost limitless market opportunities already assured by political control, preestablished commercial contacts, and other ties? Of course Victorian England was a free-trade nation! But this was not because England had by then attained to "true" capitalism. It was because England had come first on the scene with the most; because the English economy could not have functioned as the industrial, financial, and trading center of the world without free trade. Where, outside of nineteenth-century England, has this "pure," protectionless, monopoly-less capitalism existed at any time among the great powers?

This preeminence in world markets of nineteenth-century England not only explains, I believe, the free-trade character of English capitalism, but also affected the capitalisms which came to the fore later, and which, in their developmental stages, had to contend with the existing condition of English supremacy. It is significant, for example, that American capitalism, which developed unimpeded by monarchical power, and German capitalism, where the monarchical element was a factor, were both characterized by strong tendencies toward protectionism and monopolism.

In arguing that protectionism is a mere atavism, and that the logic of capitalism tends toward internationalism and free trade, Schumpeter generalizes on the basis of an atypical model and consequently misses the following basic points: that capitalism was organized along national lines and developed unevenly among the nations of the world; that this development was not smoothly upward, but was featured by fits and starts, including periods when factors lay idle and wanting employment; that finance monopolism played an increasingly key role as that development proceeded; and that these conditions made for an intensified economic rivalry among nations which was abetted rather than abated by the growing concentrations of capital within nations.

In this connection it is interesting to note that Lenin, who was writing on imperialism at about the same time as Schumpeter, also contrasts Disraeli's famous remark of 1852 (on the colonies being millstones) with his attitude some two decades later. But where Schumpeter takes the position that Disraeli seized upon the cry of Imperial Federation as a happy slogan to revive the fortunes of the Tory party, Lenin interprets this change as a symptom that British leaders were already looking uneasily about for some insurance to preserve Britain's position against the growing menace of its more dynamic and efficient young rivals now coming to the fore—Germany and the United States.

Schumpeter's brilliant dissection of British party politics in the nineteenth century may appeal more to the scholar than the crude hammerblows of Lenin. But it is Lenin's imperialism which takes account of — indeed, makes into its central feature — the headlong international scramble of the capitalist powers in the final quarter of the nineteenth century to stake out claims in Africa, to secure strategic financial positions in the Balkans and the Middle East, to outmanoeuvre and outgrab one another in the Far East, a scramble that finally culminated in World War I; while it is Schumpeter's imperialism which passes by this scramble and which views World War I as an unprovoked assault of a villainous autocracy against a democratic, peace-loving, anti-imperialist community.

Developments toward economic nationalism since World War I render Schumpeter's atavism theory of protectionism even more untenable. This period's strong and almost universal trend toward autarchy cannot possibly be understood as the revival or survival of eighteenth-century absolutism, but can be comprehended only as deriving from strains and weaknesses within the fold of international capitalism itself.

In this connection, Keynes' notes on mercantilism, demonstrating the advantages of a regulated system in stimulating output where idle factors are present, make far more sense for the period of later-day capitalism than Schumpeter's atavism theory — for Schumpeter's thesis of free trade, basing itself on the beauties of classical theory, assumes full employment, perfect competition, and complete mobility of factors, conditions hardly typical of later-day capitalism. Certainly it would not matter who built a particular railroad in Central Africa — *if* there were no special need for British, or German, or American capital to go there rather than anywhere else it chose to go; *if* there were no special stimulation to be derived by British, or German, or American heavy industry in building it; *if* there were no special advantages to British, or German, or American textile industries in selling piecegoods to the African railroad workers, since these industries could market their wares anywhere and at any time they liked. But what kind of world is Schumpeter talking about to deny these special needs — or to attribute such needs to a hangover from a former era?

III

We may now turn briefly to Schumpeter's argument that the sociology of capitalism — its social atmosphere, attitudes, and ideals — is antithetical to imperialism. Capitalism, he says, is rationalistic. It fosters democratization and individualization. It does away with blind loyalties to monarch, lord, or clan, and produces an atrophy of the martial spirit and the instinctive urge to aggression. Since capitalist rationalism stresses self-interest, and since imperialism is irrational and contrary to the interests of the majority, members of the capitalist society increasingly reject imperialism. In this rejection they are strengthened politically and morally by the tendency of capitalism to foster democratization and individualization. Furthermore, fighting is distasteful and unsuited to the bourgeois mind. The bourgeoisie, by its inherent disposition, cannot furnish the magnetic and forceful leadership needed by an imperialist state.

Now there is no question that rising capitalism leveled the weapons of rationalistic inquiry against the irrational (because outmoded) integument of feudalism, or that the development of modern science was closely linked with the rise of capitalism. But does this necessarily mean that capitalism as a system is rational? True, the individual capitalist has organized his equipment and technique of production along the most scientific lines. His bookkeeping is a triumph of cost accounting. And when he expands or curtails operations in accordance with market demands, he is certainly acting "rationally" in his own eyes. But rationally in relation to what? To a set of forces over which neither he nor anyone else can exert control, which has developed intensifying periodic crises, which keeps a significant portion of its human and capital resources in alternating states of enforced idleness, which tends to find solution more and more in production of goods that lie *outside* the "rational" mechanism of the market — namely, armaments.

The irony of a superbly rational productive apparatus standing idle while human needs go unfilled, of an awesome scientific technique producing implements of death — is it not this irony that has converted capitalism's former meliorism, optimism and faith in progress, into a bleak cynicism; which has turned capitalist culture, its art, literature, and music, increasingly away from the realism it once fostered and toward a "revolt from reason," toward a conscious glorification of the irrational, toward

feudal Catholicism, mysticism, escapism, and faddism? Is it not the "rational" capitalist era which has developed such rationalizations as racism, "the white man's burden," "manifest destiny," chauvinism, and the doctrine of "national interest"? If the world history of the last seventy-five years indicates anything, it indicates that the feudal age had no monopoly on incitements to war, that capitalism itself is quite equal to providing its own shibboleths and slogans to drag its masses into military conquest.

Much the same can be said of individualization and democratization. Early capitalism, struggling against feudal fetters, did foster these tendencies, in its own way and for its own purposes. Decadent capitalism, fostering an undemocratic concentration of economic and political power, bends the democratic process to its own ends, restricts opportunity, enforces mass attitudes, tastes, and conformities, and thereby negates its own early promises. The "individual," whom early capitalism liberated from the integrative feudal universe, is converted to a cipher. The individualization and democratization of nineteenth-century American capitalism, to cite only one specific instance, did not stand for a moment against the lords of the jingo press, whose efforts stampeded public opinion into a war with Spain in 1898 — a war that must be characterized as imperialist if the term is to mean anything.

Schumpeter presents the typical bourgeois as a man of preeminently peaceful disposition, preoccupied with his concern of making money, meekly envious of the lordly aristocracy whom he can never hope to emulate but upon whom he must depend for those qualities of leadership necessary for the functioning of the state machine. Is it not strange that this bourgeois group should, in one context, be described by the author as including the driving, ruthless, pioneering innovators, the daring organizational geniuses, the men of vision whose dynamic force propels all society along with them — and that in another context it should be described, when once outside its little circle of economic activities, as not capable of "saying boo to a goose"?

Here again is an instance of Schumpeter's seeing early capitalism as the ideal of all capitalism. Schumpeter's peaceable bourgeois did indeed exist. Balzac gives us a perfect insight into the typical early bourgeois, confined to his counting house, piling penny upon penny, once outside his shop cutting a comical and almost pathetic figure in the society of his betters. But Balzac wrote in the early nineteenth century. One need only contrast Balzac's (and Schumpeter's) bourgeois of 1830 with the captains of industry of 1890 to see how in-applicable this early type is for the period of mature capitalism.

Schumpeter's thesis defining imperialism as the expression of a warrior-class social structure is untenable as a generalized theory of imperialism. Its inadequacies show up most clearly in its application to capitalism, the attempt at such an application resulting in a distortion of the nature of capitalism, including the positing of un-acceptable supporting explanations, such as the atavism theory. Schumpeter's attempt to establish a theory true for ancient Egypt, feudal France, and twentieth-century capitalism results not in a generalized theory but in an unhistoric abstraction.

A CRITIQUE OF IMPERIALISM

WILLIAM L. LANGER

William L. Langer (1896–   ), while maintaining an eminent repu-
tation as a historian at Harvard, has served with distinction in a variety
of other capacities as well, including as Chief of Research and Analysis
Branch, Office of Strategic Services, 1942–45; assistant director of the
Central Intelligence Agency, 1950–52; and director of Harvard's Russian
Research Center and the Center for Middle Eastern Studies, since 1954.
Langer's international historical reputation was established in the early
1930's with two companion volumes on nineteenth-century diplomacy,
European Alliances and Alignments, 1871–1890 and *The Diplomacy of
Imperialism, 1890–1902*, of which the essay below is a widely read by-
product. A "middle-of-the-roader" in historical interpretation and a
historian of vast erudition, Langer is well suited both by temperament
and scholarship to evaluate the different theories of nineteenth-century
European expansion.

I T is now roughly fifty years since the beginning of that great outburst of expansive activity on the part of the Great
Powers of Europe which we have come to
call "imperialism." And it is about a generation since J. A. Hobson published his
"Imperialism: a Study," a book which has
served as the starting point for most later
discussions and which has proved a perennial inspiration for writers of the most diverse schools. A reappraisal of it is therefore
decidedly in order. The wonder is that it
has not been undertaken sooner.

Since before the outbreak of the World
War the theoretical writing on imperialism
has been very largely monopolized by the
so-called Neo-Marxians, that is, by those
who, following in the footsteps of the
master, have carried on his historical analysis from the critique of capitalism to the
study of this further phase, imperialism,
the significance of which Marx himself did
not appreciate and the very existence of
which he barely adumbrated. The Neo-
Marxians, beginning with Rudolf Hilfer-

ding and Rosa Luxemburg, have by this
time elaborated a complete theory, which
has recently been expounded in several pon-
derous German works. The theory hinges
upon the idea of the accumulation of capital, its adherents holding that imperialism
is nothing more nor less than the last stage
in the development of capitalism — the stage
in which the surplus capital resulting from
the system of production is obliged by ever
diminishing returns at home to seek new
fields for investment abroad. When this
surplus capital has transformed the whole
world and remade even the most backward
areas in the image of capitalism, the whole
economic-social system will inevitably die
of congestion.

That the classical writers of the socialistic
school derived this basic idea from Hobson's
book there can be no doubt. Lenin himself admitted, in his "Imperialism, the Latest Stage of Capitalism," that Hobson gave
"a very good and accurate description of
the fundamental economic and political
traits of imperialism," and that Hobson and

From William L. Langer, "A Critique of Imperialism," *Foreign Affairs*, XIV (October, 1935), 102–115.
Reproduced by special permission from *Foreign Affairs*, October, 1935. Copyright by the Council on
Foreign Relations, Inc., New York.

Hilferding had said the essentials on the subject. This, then, has been the most fruitful contribution of Hobson's essay. When we examine his ideas on this subject we refer indirectly to the larger part of the writing on imperialism since his day.

As a matter of pure economic theory it is most difficult to break down the logic of the accumulation theory. It is a fact that since the middle of the last century certain countries — first England, then France, Germany and the United States — have exported large amounts of capital, and that the financial returns from these investments in many instances came to overshadow completely the income derived by the lending countries from foreign trade. It is also indisputable that industry embarked upon the road to concentration and monopoly, that increased efficiency in production led to larger profits and to the amassing of ever greater surpluses of capital. We must recognize further that, as a general rule, the return from investments abroad was distinctly above the return on reinvestment in home industry. In other words, the postulates of the socialist theory undoubtedly existed. There is no mentionable reason why the development of the capitalist system should not have had the results attributed to it.

But, as it happens, the actual course of history refutes the thesis. The course of British investment abroad shows that there was a very considerable export of capital before 1875, that is, during the climax of anti-imperialism in England. Between 1875 and 1895, while the tide of imperialism was coming to the full, there was a marked falling off of foreign investment. Capital export was then resumed on a large scale in the years before the war, though England was, in this period, already somewhat disillusioned by the outcome of the South African adventure and rather inclined to be skeptical about imperialism. Similar observations hold true of the United States. If the promulgation of the Monroe Doctrine was an act of imperialism, where was the export of capital which ought to have

been its condition? Let us concede that the war with Spain was an imperialist episode. At that time the United States was still a debtor nation, importing rather than exporting capital. In Russia, too, the heyday of imperialism coincided with a period of heavy borrowing rather than of lending.

There is this further objection to be raised against the view of Hobson and his Neo-Marxian followers, that the export of capital seems to have little direct connection with territorial expansion. France, before the war, had plenty of capital to export, and some of her earliest and most vigorous imperialists, like Jules Ferry, declared that she required colonies in order to have adequate fields for the placement of this capital. But when France had secured colonies, she did not send her capital to them. By far the larger part of her exported funds went to Russia, Rumania, Spain and Portugal, Egypt and the Ottoman Empire. In 1902 only two or two and a half billion francs out of a total foreign investment of some 30 or 35 billion francs was placed in the colonies. In 1913 Britain had more money invested in the United States than in any colony or other foreign country. Less than half of her total export of capital had been to other parts of the Empire. The United States put more capital into the development of Canada than did England; and when, after the war, the United States became a great creditor nation, 43 percent of her investment was in Latin America, 27 percent in Canada and Newfoundland, and 22 percent in European countries. What she sent to her colonies was insignificant. Or let us take Germany, which in 1914 had about 25 billion marks placed abroad. Of this total only three percent was invested in Asia and Africa, and of that three percent only a small part in her colonies. Pre-war Russia was a great imperialist power, but Russia had to borrow from France the money invested in her Far Eastern projects. In our own day two of the most outspokenly imperialist powers, Japan and Italy, are both nations poor in capital. Whatever the urge that drives them to expansion, it cannot be the need for the export of capital.

At the height of the imperialist tide, let us say from 1885 to 1914, there was much less talk among the advocates of expansion about the need for foreign investment fields than about the need for new markets and for the safeguarding of markets from the tariff restrictions of competitors. It is certain that in the opinion of contemporaries that was the mainspring of the whole movement. But this economic explanation, like the other, has not been borne out by the actual developments. Very few colonies have done even half of their trading with the mother country and many have done less. Taken in the large it can be proved statistically that the colonial trade has always played a relatively unimportant part in the total foreign commerce of the great industrial nations. These nations have always been each other's best customers and no amount of rivalry and competition has prevented their trade from following, not the flag, but the price-list. The position of Canada within the British Empire did not prevent her from levying tariffs against British goods, nor from developing exceedingly close economic relations with the United States. In the pre-war period German commerce with the British possessions was expanding at a relatively higher rate than was Britain's.

If one must have an economic interpretation of imperialism, one will probably find its historical evolution to have been something like this: In the days of England's industrial preëminence she was, by the very nature of the case, interested in free trade. In the palmiest days of Cobdenism she exported manufactured goods to the four corners of the earth, but she exported also machinery and other producers' goods, thereby preparing the way for the industrialization of the continental nations and latterly of other regions of the world. In order to protect their infant industries from British competition, these new industrial Powers threw over the teachings of the Manchester school and began to set up tariffs. The result was that the national markets were set aside, to a large extent, for home industry. British trade was driven to seek new markets, where the process was repeated. But the introduction of protective tariffs had this further effect, that it made possible the organization of cartels and trusts, that is, the concentration of industry, the increase of production and the lowering of costs. Surplus goods and low prices caused the other industrial Powers likewise to look abroad for additional markets, and, while this development was taking place, technological improvements were making transportation and communication safer and more expeditious. The exploration of Africa at that time was probably a pure coincidence, but it contributed to the movement toward trade and expansion and the growth of a world market. Fear that the newly opened areas of the world might be taken over by others and then enclosed in tariff walls led directly to the scramble for territory in Asia and Africa.

The socialist writers would have us believe that concentration in industry made for monopoly and that the banks, undergoing the same process of evolution, were, through their connection with industry, enabled to take over control of the whole capitalist system. They were the repositories of the surplus capital accumulated by a monopolistic system and they were therefore the prime movers in the drive for imperial expansion, their problem being to find fields for the investment of capital. This is an argument which does violence to the facts as they appear historically. The socialist writers almost to a man argue chiefly from the example of Germany, where cartelization came early and where the concentration of banking and the control of industry by the banks went further than in most countries. But even in Germany the movement towards overseas expansion came before the growth of monopoly and the amalgamation of the banks. In England, the imperialist country *par excellence*, there was no obvious connection between the two phenomena. The trust movement came late and never went as far as in Germany. The same was true of the consolidation of the banking system. One of the perennial complaints in England was the lack of proper coördination between the banks and industry. To a certain extent the English exported capital because the machinery for foreign investment was better than the organization for home investment. In the United States, to be sure, there was already a pronounced concentration of industry when the great outburst of imperialism came in the last years of the past century, but in general the trust movement ran parallel to the movement for territorial expansion. In any event, it would be hard to disprove the contention that the growth of world trade and the world market brought on the tendency toward better organization and concentration in industry, rather than the reverse. It is obvious not only that one large unit can manufacture more cheaply than many small ones, but that it can act more efficiently in competition with others in the world market.

But this much is clear — that territorial control of extra-European territory solved neither the trade problem nor the question of surplus capital. The white colonies, which were the best customers, followed their own economic interests and not even tariff restrictions could prevent them from doing so. In the backward, colored, tropical colonies, which could be more easily controlled and exploited, it proved difficult to develop a market, because of the low purchasing power of the natives. The question of raw materials, of which so much has always been made, also remained open. The great industrial countries got but a fraction of their raw materials from the colonies, and the colonies themselves continued to show a tendency to sell their products in the best market. As for the export of capital, that continued to flow in an ever broader stream, not because the opportunities for investment at home were exhausted, but because the return from foreign investment was apt to be better and because, in many cases, foreign investment

was the easier course. Capital flowed from the great industrial countries of Europe, but it did not flow to their colonies. The United States and Canada, Latin America (especially the Argentine) and even old countries like Austria-Hungary and Russia, got the bulk of it. The export of capital necessarily took the form of the extension of credit, which in turn implied the transfer of goods. Not infrequently the granting of loans was made conditional on trade concessions by the borrowing country. So we come back to the question of trade and tariffs. In a sense the export of capital was nothing but a device to stimulate trade and to circumvent tariff barriers, which brings us back to the coincidence of the movement for protection and the movement toward imperialism.

This may seem like an oversimplified explanation and it probably is. Some may argue that imperialism is more than a movement toward territorial expansion and that financial imperialism in particular lays the iron hand of control on many countries supposedly independent. But if you try to divorce imperialism from territorial control you will get nowhere. Practically all writers on the subject have been driven to the conclusion that the problem cannot be handled at all unless you restrict it in this way. When Hobson wrote on imperialism, he had reference to the great spectacle of a few Powers taking over tremendous areas in Africa and Asia. Imperialism is, in a sense, synonymous with the appropriation by the western nations of the largest part of the rest of the world. If you take it to be anything else, you will soon be lost in nebulous concepts and bloodless abstractions. If imperialism is to mean any vague interference of traders and bankers in the affairs of other countries, you may as well extend it to cover any form of influence. You will have to admit cultural imperialism, religious imperialism, and what not. Personally I prefer to stick by a measurable, manageable concept.

But even though Hobson's idea, that imperialism "is the endeavor of the great controllers of industry to broaden the channel for the flow of their surplus wealth by seeking foreign markets and foreign investments to take off the goods and capital they cannot sell or use at home," proved to be the most stimulating and fertile of his arguments, he had the very correct idea that imperialism was also a "medley of aims and feelings." He had many other contributory explanations of the phenomenon. For example, he was keenly aware of the relationship between democracy and imperialism. The enfranchisement of the working classes and the introduction of free education had brought the rank and file of the population into the political arena. One result of this epoch-making change was the rise of the so-called yellow press, which catered to the common man's love of excitement and sensationalism. Northcliffe was one of the first to sense the value of imperialism as a "talking point." Colonial adventure and far-away conflict satisfied the craving for excitement of the industrial and white-collar classes which had to find some outlet for their "spectatorial lust." The upper crust of the working class, as Lenin admitted, was easily converted to the teaching of imperialism and took pride in the extension of empire.

No doubt this aspect of the problem is important. The mechanization of humanity in an industrial society is a phenomenon with which we have become all too familiar, and every thoughtful person now recognizes the tremendous dangers inherent in the powers which the demagogue can exercise through the press, the motion picture and the radio. In Hobson's day propaganda was still carried on primarily through the press, but later developments were already foreshadowed in the activities of a Northcliffe or a Hearst. Hobson himself was able to show how, during the war in South Africa, the English press took its information from the South African press, which had been brought very largely under the control of Rhodes and his associates. Even at that time Hobson and others were pointing out how imperialistic capital was influencing not only the press, but the pulpit and the universities. Indeed, Hobson went so far as to claim that the great inert mass of the population, who saw the tangled maze of world movements through dim and bewildered eyes, were the inevitable dupes of able, organized interests who could lure or scare or drive them into any convenient course.

Recognizing as we do that control of the public mind involves the most urgent political problems of the day, it is nevertheless important to point out that there is nothing inexorable about the connection of propaganda and imperialism. Even if you admit that a generation ago moneyed interests believed that imperialism was to their advantage, that these interests exercised a far-reaching control over public opinion, and that they used this control to dupe the common man into support of imperial ventures, it is obvious that at some other time these same interests might have different ideas with regard to their own welfare, just as it is evident that public opinion may be controlled by some other agency — the modern dictator, for example.

But the same thing is not true of another influence upon which Hobson laid great stress, namely the biological conception of politics and international relations. During the last years of the nineteenth century the ideas of "social Darwinism," as it was called, carried everything before them. Darwin's catchwords — the struggle for existence and the survival of the fittest — which he himself always refused to apply to the social organism, were snapped up by others who were less scrupulous, and soon became an integral part of popular and even official thought on foreign affairs. It not only served to justify the ruthless treatment of the "backward" races and the carving up *in spe* of the Portuguese, Spanish, Ottoman and Chinese Empires and of other "dying nations," as Lord Salisbury called them, but it put the necessary imprimatur on the ideas of conflict between the great imperialistic Powers themselves, and supplied a divine sanction for expansion. It was currently believed, in the days of exuberant imperialism, that the world would soon be the preserve of the great states — the British, the American and the Russian — and it was deduced from this belief that survival in the struggle for existence was in itself adequate evidence of superiority and supernatural appointment. The British therefore looked upon their empire as a work of the divine will, while the Americans and Russians were filled with the idea of a manifest destiny. It will be at once apparent that glorification of war and joy in the conflict was intimately connected with the evolutionary mentality. Hobson, the most determined of anti-imperialists, was finally driven to define the whole movement as "a depraved choice of national life, imposed by self-seeking interests which appeal to the lusts of quantitative acquisitiveness and of forceful domination surviving in a nation from early centuries of animal struggle for existence."[1]

The last phrases of this quotation will serve to lead us to the consideration of what has proved to be another fruitful thought of Hobson. He speaks, in one place, of imperialism as a sociological atavism, a remnant of the roving instinct, just as hunting and sport are left-overs of the physical struggle for existence. This idea of the roving instinct has made but little appeal to later writers, but the basic interpretation of imperialism as an atavism underlies the ingenious and highly intelligent essay of Joseph Schumpeter, "Zur Soziologie der Imperialismen," the only work from the bourgeois side which has had anything like the influence exerted by the writers of the socialist school. Schumpeter, who is an eminent economist, worked out a most convincing argument to prove that imperialism has nothing to do with capitalism, and that it is certainly not a development of capitalism. Capitalism, he holds, is by nature opposed to expansion, war, armaments and professional militarism, and im-

perialism is nothing but an atavism, one of those elements of the social structure which cannot be explained from existing conditions, but only from the conditions of the past. It is, in other words, a hangover from a preceding economic order. Imperialism antedates capitalism, going back at least to the time of the Assyrians and Egyptians. It is, according to Schumpeter, the disposition of a state to forceful expansion without any special object and without a definable limit. Conquests are desired not so much because of their advantages, which are often questionable, but merely for the sake of conquest, success and activity.

Schumpeter's theory is in some ways extravagant, but it has served as the starting point for some very interesting speculation, especially among German scholars of the liberal persuasion. It is now fairly clear, I think, that the Neo-Marxian critics have paid far too little attention to the imponderable, psychological ingredients of imperialism. The movement may, without much exaggeration, be interpreted not only as an atavism, as a remnant of the days of absolute monarchy and mercantilism, when it was to the interest of the prince to increase his territory and the number of his subjects, but also as an aberration, to be classed with the extravagances of nationalism. Just as nationalism can drive individuals to the point of sacrificing their very lives for the purposes of the state, so imperialism has driven them to the utmost exertions and the extreme sacrifice, even though the stake might be only some little known and at bottom valueless part of Africa or Asia. In the days when communication and economic interdependence have made the world one in so many ways, men still interpret international relations in terms of the old cabinet policies, they are still swayed by out-moded, feudalistic ideas of honor and prestige.

In a sense, then, you can say that there is, in every people, a certain indefinable national energy, which may find expression in a variety of ways.

[1] In the last paragraph of his *Imperialism. A Study*. [Editor's note]

As a general rule great domestic crises and outbursts of expansion follow each other in the history of the world. In many of the continental countries of Europe, and for that matter in our own country, great internal problems were fought out in the period before 1870. The energies which, in Germany and Italy, went into the victory of the national cause, soon began to project themselves beyond the frontiers. While the continental nations were settling great issues between them, England sat "like a bloated Quaker, rubbing his hands at the roaring trade" he was carrying on. In those days the British cared very little for their empire. Many of them would have felt relieved if the colonies had broken away without a fuss. But, says Egerton, the best-known historian of British colonial policy, when the Germans and the French began to show an interest in colonial expansion, then the British began to think that there must be some value as yet undiscovered in the colonies. They not only started a movement to bind the colonies and the mother country more closely together, but they stretched out their hands for more. In the end they, who had the largest empire to begin with, got easily the lion's share of the yet unappropriated parts of the world. Some thought they were engaged in the fulfilment of a divine mission to abolish slavery, to spread the gospel, to clothe and educate the heathen. Others thought they were protecting the new markets from dangerous competitors, securing their supply of raw materials, or finding new fields for investment. But underlying the whole imperial outlook there was certainly more than a little misapprehension of economics, much self-delusion and self-righteousness, much misapplication of evolutionary teaching and above all much of the hoary tradition of honor, prestige, power and even plain combativeness. Imperialism always carries with it the connotation of the *Imperator* and of the tradition of rule. It is bound up with conscious or subconscious ideas of force, of brutality, of ruthlessness. It was these traits and tendencies that were so vividly expressed in the poetry and stories of Kipling, and it was his almost uncanny ability to sense the emotions of his time and people that made him the greatest apostle of imperialism.

We shall not go far wrong, then, if we stress the psychological and political factors in imperialism as well as its economic and intellectual elements. It was, of course, connected closely with the great changes in the social structure of the western world, but it was also a projection of nationalism beyond the boundaries of Europe, a projection on a world scale of the time-honored struggle for power and for a balance of power as it had existed on the Continent for centuries. The most casual perusal of the literature of imperialism will reveal the continued potency of these atavistic motives. In a recent number of this very journal a leading Italian diplomat, explaining the policy of the Duce, recurred again and again to the failure of the other countries to appreciate the fact that Italy is a young and active country "animated by new spiritual values." By the much-decried Corfu episode of 1923, Mussolini, to give a concrete example, "called Europe's attention to the respect due to the new Italy and to the reawakened energies of the Italian people." In the present Ethiopian crisis there is not very much suggestion of economic or civilizing motives on the part of the Italians; rather the Duce holds before his followers the prospect of revenge for the defeat at Adua (reminiscent of Britain's thirst to avenge Gordon) and promises them a glorious future. Not long ago he spoke to a group of veterans among the ruins of ancient Rome and told them that every stone surrounding them should remind them that Rome once dominated the world by the wisdom of her rule and the might of her arms and that "nothing forbids us to believe that what was our destiny yesterday may again become our destiny tomorrow." In much the same spirit an eminent Japanese statesman expressed himself recently in FOREIGN AFFAIRS: "As soon as the Meiji Restoration lifted the ban on foreign intercourse, the long-pent-up energy of our race was released, and with fresh outlook and enthusiasm the nation has made swift progress. When you know this historical background and understand this overflowing vitality of our race, you will see the impossibility of compelling us to stay still within the confines of our little island home. We are destined to grow and expand overseas." It is the same emphasis given by the Italian diplomat to the need for an outlet for surplus energies.

It is, of course, true that both Italy and Japan have a serious population problem and that Japan, at any rate, has an economic argument to back her imperialistic enterprises in Manchuria and China. But it has been shown long ago that the acquisition of new territory has no direct bearing on the population problem and that emigrants go where their interest calls them, not where their governments would like to have them go. As for Japan's economic needs, it may at least be questioned whether she would not be better off if she avoided political and military commitments in China. Her cheap goods have made very extensive inroads in all the markets of the world, and her eventual conquest of the whole Chinese market is perhaps inevitable. Far from having gained much from her recent policy, she has had to face boycotts and other forms of hostility. In this case, certainly, one might debate whether the game is worth the candle.

Baron Wakatsuki,[2] whose statement is quoted above, was careful to avoid mention of a factor in Japanese imperialism which, as every well-informed person knows, is probably the real explanation of Japanese policy. After the Meiji Restoration it was more the exuberance and bellicosity of the military caste in Japan than the enthusiasm of the country at large which determined the policy of the government. If one reads modern Japanese history aright one will find that from 1870 onward the military classes were constantly pressing upon the government for action in Korea. Only with the greatest difficulty did the civil authori-

ties stave off this pressure. In 1894 the Tokyo government more or less rushed into the war with China in order to avoid a dangerous domestic crisis. In other words, the ideas of honor and patriotism were appealed to in order to divert attention from the parliamentary conflict which was then raging. After the Japanese victory it was the military men who, against the better judgment of men like Count Ito and Baron Mutsu, insisted on the cession of the Liaotung Peninsula, which netted Japan nothing but the intervention of Russia, Germany, and France. We need not pursue this subject in all its minute details. The point I want to make is that in the case of Japan, as in the case of many other countries, it is easier to show that the military and official classes are a driving force behind the movement for expansion than to show that a clique of nefarious bankers or industrialists is the determining factor. Business interests may have an interest in the acquisition of territory, or they may not. But military and official classes almost always have. War is, for the soldiers, a profession, and it is no mere chance that war and imperialism are so commonly lumped together. For officials, expansion means new territories to govern and new jobs to be filled.

Hobson, with his pronouncedly economic approach to the problem, held that "the struggle for markets, the greater eagerness of producers to sell than of consumers to buy, is the crowning proof of a false economy of distribution," of which imperialism is the fruit. The remedy, he thought, lay in "social reform." "There is no necessity to open up new foreign markets," he maintained; "the home markets are capable of indefinite expansion." These contentions sound familiar enough in this day of world depression. Whether the home markets are capable of indefinite expansion is a question on which the economic internationalists and the advocates of autarchy hold different opinions. The interesting thing for us to consider, however, is the fact that movements towards autarchy should have developed at all and that so much stress

---

[2] Baron Wakatsuki was premier of Japan, 1926–27. [Editor's note]

should now be laid upon the problems of redistribution of wealth, of building up purchasing power, and, in general, of domestic social reform. The current of activity has shifted distinctly from expansion to revolution, peaceful or violent. Perhaps it may be argued from this that the socialist thesis regarding imperialism is now being proved; that capitalism has already transformed the backward areas to such an extent that the markets are ruined, and that the capitalist system is rapidly choking. This view might be acceptable if it were not for the fact that the colonies and backward areas are still very far from developed and if it were not for the further fact that before the depression the colonial trade with the older countries was steadily increasing. In the last five years, to be sure, international commerce has sunk to an unbelievably low point, but the difficulty has been chiefly with the trade between the great industrial Powers themselves. It is quite conceivable that the crisis is primarily due to the special situation arising from the World War and that the root of the trouble lies in the impossibility of fitting tremendous international payments into the existing framework of trade relations. The fantastic tariff barriers which have been set up on all sides have simply aggravated a situation which has been developing since the teachings of Cobdenism first began to fall into disrepute.

But whatever the true explanation of our present difficulties, very few voices are raised in favor of a solution by the methods of imperialism. Indeed, the movement toward autarchy is in a way a negation of imperialism. Economically we have been disillusioned about imperialism. We have learned that colonies do not pay. Britain's expenditure for the defense of the empire alone is enormous, yet she has never yet devised a method by which anything like a commensurate return could be secured. The French military outlay on the colonies in 1913 was more than five hundred million francs, at a time when the entire trade of France with her colonies came to hardly

three times that figure. Similar statistics could be quoted for Germany, and it is a well-known fact that the colonies of both Spain and Portugal were much more of a liability than an asset.

In the same way it has turned out that foreign investments of capital are not all that they were expected to be. The higher returns from colonial investments have often been counterbalanced by the greater insecurity that went with them. European countries had more than one opportunity to learn the lesson even before the war. We need only recall the Argentine fiasco of 1890 and the wildcat Kaffir Boom in South African securities in 1895 as classical examples of what might happen. But of course all these instances are completely dwarfed by the experiences of the postwar — or perhaps better, the pre-depression decade. Foreign investments have caused acute international tensions and have resulted in phenomena like American dollar diplomacy in Latin America. The expenditure has been immense and what has been salvaged has been unimpressive enough. The nations of the world are still on the lookout for markets, as they have been for centuries, but the peoples of the world have become more or less convinced that the markets, if they can be got at all, can be got only by the offering of better and cheaper goods and not by occupation, political control or forceful exploitation. As for foreign investments, no one has any stomach for them and most of those fortunate enough to have money to invest would be glad to learn of a safe investment at home. The assurance of needed sources for raw materials is as much if not more of a problem today than it was a generation ago, but there is little sense in taking over the expensive administration of tropical or other territory to guarantee a source of raw materials, because somehow or other it usually turns out that the other fellow has the materials that you want, and it has long since become obvious that the idea of controlling sources of all the materials you may need is a snare and a delusion. . . .

FOREIGN INVESTMENT AND
FOREIGN EXPANSION

EUGENE STALEY

Eugene Staley (1906–   ) has combined an academic career (including positions at the Fletcher School of Law and Diplomacy and Stanford University) with that of an economic adviser. He has traveled overseas on projects for UNRRA, the Ford Foundation, and U. S. government agencies. His book, *War and the Private Investor*, examines, by means of case studies of particular areas, the relation between governmental and private involvement in international investments before the First World War. Staley's conclusions on the relation between investment and political expansion, as the reader will see, give some comfort to both economic and noneconomic interpretations of the period.

I F we were to engage in a thorough investigation to ascertain inductively, on the basis of specific, historical materials rather than by the untested application of any dogma or doctrine, what factors have contributed to the development of expansionism in each of the great powers and what has been the rôle of private capital among these factors, it would require at least one volume in itself to present the relevant evidence and to analyze it critically. Even then, for most countries, the evidence would not be conclusive; that is, it would be of a sort that competent and objectively minded persons could still interpret differently in important aspects. This inheres in the nature of the question under discussion. Perhaps the causation of complicated social phenomena like expansionism can never be determined with certainty. Be that as it may, despite these reservations there are two conclusions which seem to emerge with sufficient distinctness so that they deserve mention here. First, the investment pressure in which we are interested cannot be regarded as an indispensable

element in the causation of expansionism, for certain modern nations where such pressure has been absent or minimal have nevertheless developed most vigorous outward drives of a sort which we must accept as falling within our definition, since they have involved the use of investments as tools and have led to investment friction with other powers. Second, investment pressure has been a factor in the origin of expansionism in certain other countries, to a degree impossible to evaluate accurately, but differing from country to country and apparently quite important in some. In all such cases it has been intertwined with other factors of the most diverse kinds. A brief amplification of these two conclusions will bring to a close this chapter on investment conflicts between capital-exporting countries.

The pre-war histories of Russia and Italy lend no support whatever to the hypothesis that the pressure of "surplus capital" for investment abroad is an essential element in the origin of modern national expansionism. Tsarist Russia was capital-poor, a heavy borrower when possible, and yet it sprawled over Northern Asia, contested Korea and Manchuria with Japan, sought to extend its sway southward to Constantinople, and engaged in such an aggressive politico-economic penetration of Persia that England was alarmed for the safety of India. These were typical activities of the sort which has been called "capitalistic imperialism." Investments which were private in form, but really heavily subsidized by the Tsarist government, served as tools of penetration; they included banks, railroads, road construction, forestry companies, shipping and trading companies, and also loans to weaker states. Russia engaged actively in the scramble for concessions in the Far East and in the Middle East. And yet Russia had no "surplus capital" in any reasonable sense of that term; Russia had very little capital at all and borrowed heavily from abroad. Nor were Russian financiers putting pressure upon the government to get them investment opportunities abroad; the government was pressing the financiers, subsidizing them, to create political stakes abroad. Much of the capital used as a Russian diplomatic tool was borrowed in France. Lest it be suggested that Russian expansionism was therefore an expression of the outward push of French "surplus capital" it is well to point out that Russian governments had been engaging in expansionist politics for decades before the first loan was floated in France. The causes of Russian expansionism have to be sought in political ambition, dynastic megalomania, military lust for conquest. Capital was distinctly a tool, not a cause.

The case of Italy is only slightly less clear than that of Tsarist Russia. Italy, too, was a nation poor in capital, borrowing abroad for its own needs. Yet it engaged in the struggle for acquisition of territory and spheres of influence which characterized the decades before the World War. A rising spirit of nationalism seeking to assert itself in the world, the quest for prestige and glory, were more effective causes of Italian conquest in Tripoli, the establish-

ment of colonies elsewhere on the African coast, the attempt to extend Italian influence over Abyssinia, and the dispute over Tunis with France, than were any investment factors. The capital which served as a tool of penetration in Tunis and Tripoli had to be pushed in and subsidized. The opportunity to participate slightly in the Bagdad Railway enterprise, secured for Italy by its diplomats for political reasons, actually had to be taken up by so-called Italian capital of Greek origin. Italy's aggressive expansionist tendencies before the World War developed without significant pressure from opportunity-seeking capital.

It can surely be concluded from these cases that the existence of "surplus" investment capital pressing for opportunities abroad is not a *necessary* element in the origin of nationalistic imperialism, colonialism, or — in the general term used here — expansionism. On the other hand, the quest for desirable investment opportunities has undoubtedly been a factor of varying magnitude in the development of expansionism on the part of other powers. In France, Jules Ferry and other expansionists believed (or at least said, as an argument for their colonial policy) that investment opportunities were needed abroad. Propaganda of this sort came primarily from statesmen and others who were already zealous colonialists, however, not from the bankers and would-be investors themselves. Doubtless it is part of the duty of a statesman to anticipate the needs of the business community and to make them vocal and effective in national policy even before the business community is conscious of them; in this sense French expansionism received part of its impetus from a desire for investment opportunities abroad. It is worth noting, however, that investments actually made in colonies were a small part of French capital exports before the war. The major factors in French expansionism appear to have been such things as these: the conviction that trade outlets were necessary for the industrial development of the country, coupled with the rise of protectionist tendencies in markets all over the world; the impulse to seek prestige, glory, a great place in the world, for the French nation; the desire to recover the injury to national pride inflicted in 1871; the conviction that France had a mission to spread its culture abroad. The desire for investment opportunities was present, at least in the minds of statesmen, but it was hardly among the most effective causes of French expansionism.

The interests of British private investors scattered over most of the world, especially investments connected with trade, undoubtedly contributed mightily to the resurgence of British expansionism in the late nineteenth century. Their mere existence tended to turn business and political interests outward; they provided ready footholds for political operations at almost any point on the earth's surface without the necessity for creating "economic" interests out of whole cloth, as the Russians had to do; they were characteristically accompanied, unlike the investments of the French, by outposts of home enterprises and by personnel from home, which made their political significance quite different. The tendency of private capital to seek out new opportunities abroad was, therefore, an important element in modern British expansionism, along with other important factors, such as the long and still active tradition of colonialism, the naval tradition, the influence of the colonial official class, the quest of careers by younger sons of the aristocracy, missionary enterprise, the search for export markets, and the psychic satisfaction which comes from seeing one's own country cover a larger and larger portion of the world map.

The origin of German expansionism offers the most interesting case of all, for the influences at work came to a focus in shaping the policy of one dominant statesman, Bismarck. In the forces which played upon Bismarck, inducing the famous shift from his earlier maxim that Germany had only continental interests to his later studied attempt to promote German expansion in Africa and the South Seas, one sees reflected the social forces which were molding the destiny of the nation. Did the interests and influence of those who wished to place private capital profitably abroad have an important part in this shift? The answer is that they did. The powerful influence of Bismarck's banker friends, von Hansemann and Bleichröder, was exerted in favor of a colonial policy, and the practical enterprises of great merchants and shippers like Godeffroy and Woermann furnished the immediate occasions for early demonstration of the new state attitude. As in all the other cases, however, investment interests seeking opportunities and protection represented but one among a number of significant factors in the rise of expansionism. Probably the single most important consideration influencing Bismarck resulted from the rise of protectionism in the latter part of the nineteenth century and its application by other powers to their possessions. The rise of protectionism meant that a nation without colonies would have to fear exclusion from markets for its industries, limitation of trading and investment opportunities, unless it, too, entered the race for possessions and spheres of influence abroad. In the last analysis, however, even in Germany where economic forces were particularly evident in the origin of expansionist tendencies, the colonial movement was most easily justified in the eyes of the people on the basis of patriotic pride and national prestige.

The annexation of Hawaii by the United States was due in large part to the activities of American plantation owners — therefore, of private investment interests. Their main economic interest, however, was in obtaining tariff preferences for their products in the United States; so that here, too, the protectionist policy of nations was an important factor. Furthermore, the economic interests of the Hawaiian investors did not suffice in themselves to bring about annexation; after at first refusing to take over the islands, the government of the United States finally did so in the nationalistic enthusiasm aroused by the Spanish-American War. The causes of this war, and of the expansionism exhibited in connection with it, have been laid at the door of private investment interests — on the whole, erroneously. Their rôle was slight compared with that of the interests of the "yellow" press and of other internal influences in American life which made for chauvinism. Certainly, investment interests in the Caribbean countries have recently contributed significantly to American political dominance there, though strategic interests connected with naval power, defense of the Panama Canal, and the traditional policy of the Monroe Doctrine were probably more important in turning the political attention of the United States government to the region. The Caribbean seems to offer one of the best illustrations of the "balance-wheel" effect of private investments. Coming in, on the whole, after the political interest, they have tended to make it more intense and permanent. American political interests in the Far East were closely connected with trade from the first, and more recently investments have come to share the importance of trade in conditioning policy. But there has been no important tendency for the United States to adopt an expansionist program there. The conclusion with respect to the United States must be much like those reached for France, England, and Germany: private foreign investments have figured in national expansionism, but as one among many factors, some of which have been more important than the investment influence.

Finally, Japan must be considered. Certainly, in this case, though the forces producing Japanese expansionism may be largely economic in the broad sense of that term, the direct influence of private profit-motivated enterprise seeking either investment opportunities or protection abroad has not been a very significant item in the development of that expansionism. Rather, Japan, like Russia and Italy, has borrowed abroad and pushed subsidized enterprises into coveted territory in order to establish political stakes. Perhaps Japanese statesmen have been influenced in part by the consideration that some time in the future the country will be in need of profitable outlets for "surplus capital" abroad, but even this must be counted a minor factor in comparison with such forces as the concern over population pressure on the standard of living, the belief that raw materials lacking in Japan must be secured by national expansion abroad, the social and political prestige of the military class, and nationalistic pride such as that which has driven forward the colonial enterprises of other states.

BASES OF A NEW NATIONAL IMPERIALISM

CARLTON J. H. HAYES

A gifted and prolific historian, Carlton J. H. Hayes (1882–   ) has been associated with Columbia University since 1900, when he entered it as an undergraduate. By the time of his retirement in 1950, Hayes was Seth Low Professor of History, having in the meantime been a visiting professor to a number of universities and having served as the United States ambassador to Spain from 1942 to 1945. Hayes' best-known books, including some distinguished texts, have been in the fields of nationalism and of general European history. *A Generation of Materialism, 1871–1900*, one of *The Rise of Modern Europe* series, edited by W. L. Langer, combines these two interests in both scope and approach. It has been one of Hayes' most highly regarded books.

SYNCHRONIZING with the revival of protective tariffs and the extension of socializing legislation toward the close of the 1870's, was a tremendous outburst of imperialistic interest and activity. The outburst was common to all great powers of Europe (except Austria-Hungary); and it was so potent that during the next three decades greater progress was made toward subjecting the world to European domination than had been made during three centuries previous.

This may seem odd in view of the fact that the immediately preceding era of Liberal ascendancy, say from the 1840's into the 1870's, had witnessed a marked decline of European imperialism. There had been, to be sure, some spasmodic additions to British India, some scattered efforts of Napoleon III to resuscitate a colonial empire for France, some continuing Russian expansion in central and northeastern Asia. Although China and Japan had been forcefully opened to European (and American) trade, the opening had been for practically everybody on free and equal terms and had

been unattended by any considerable expropriation of territory. The surviving far-flung British Empire had ceased to be an exclusive preserve for British merchants since the 1840's, and in 1861 France had freely admitted to her colonies the commerce of all nations. In 1870–1871 European colonialism appeared to be approaching its nadir. Gladstone was prime minister of Great Britain, and he was notoriously a "Little Englander." The provisional French government so slightly esteemed the colonies it had inherited that it offered them all to Bismarck at the end of the Franco-Prussian War if only he would spare Alsace-Lorraine. Bismarck spurned the offer, as he had recently refused Portugal's offer to sell him Mozambique. A colonial policy for Germany, he said, "would be just like the silken sables of Polish noble families who have no shirts."

A favorite explanation of why European imperialism turned abruptly within a decade from nadir to apogee, has been the economic. It was advanced originally by publicists and statesmen to win the support

From *A Generation of Materialism, 1871–1900* by Carlton J. H. Hayes. Copyright 1941 by Harper & Brothers, N. Y., pp. 216–229. By permission of the publishers. Kipling's verse by permission of Mrs. George Bambridge, Macmillan Company of Canada, Ltd., Methuen and Co. Ltd., and Doubleday & Company, Inc.

of business interests for imperialistic policies, and it received classical treatment, at the time of the Boer War, by John A. Hobson. Latterly it has been taken up by Marxian writers and integrated with their dogma of materialistic determinism, so that the argument now runs in this wise: Imperialism is an inevitable phase in the evolution of capitalism, a phase in which surplus capital, accumulated by the exploitation of domestic labor, is obliged by diminishing returns at home to find new outlets for investment abroad. Hence it seeks non-industrialized areas ever farther afield where it may dispose of surplus manufactures, obtain needed raw materials, invest surplus capital, and exploit cheap native labor. The resulting "new imperialism," unlike the old, is not primarily a colonizing or a simply commercial imperialism, but rather an investing one in regions ill-adapted to European settlement. Conditions are alleged to have been ripe for it about 1880, when tariff protection restricted customary markets of European capitalists and impelled them to seek new ones.

Doubtless large-scale mechanized industry, with accompanying improvement of transportation facilities, did immensely stimulate an ever-widening quest for markets where surplus manufactures might be disposed of, necessary raw materials procured, and lucrative investments made. Nor can there be any doubt that by the 1870's, when industrialization on the Continent was beginning seriously to vie with England's, the quest was being as eagerly pursued by commercial and banking houses of Hamburg and Bremen, Marseilles and Paris, as by those of London and Liverpool. In Germany, for example, at the very time when Bismarck was disdaining the French proffer of colonies, his banking friends, Bleichröder and Hansemann, were helping to finance distant trade ventures of various Hanseatic firms — O'Swald's in East Africa, Woermann's in West Africa, Godeffroy's in Samoa and other South Sea islands. In 1880 some 335,000 marks' worth of German goods were shipped to West Africa alone, while 6,735,000 marks' worth of African products entered the port of Hamburg.

Yet the only novel feature of all this was a relatively greater importation of tropical and sub-tropical products and hence a special concern with Africa, southern Asia, the Indies, and Oceania. Surplus manufactures from industrialized countries of Europe, even after the imposition of protective tariffs, still found export markets principally within that Continent or in temperate zones outside, notably in America, Australasia, northern India, and the Far East. What actually started the economic push into the "Dark Continent" and the sun-baked islands of the Pacific was not so much an over-production of factory goods in Europe as an undersupply of raw materials. Cotton grew finer in Egypt than in the United States, and with the partial cutting off of the latter's copious supply by the American Civil War it was but natural that dealers in raw cotton should enter the Egyptian field and raise its yield ninefold during the next twenty years. Rubber was now needed also, and it could be got from the Congo and from Malaysia more cheaply and plentifully than from Brazil. Copra, with its useful oil, was to be had in the South Sea islands, and the Godeffroy firm at Hamburg made a specialty of going for it. Tin was essential for the new canning industry, and gold, for measuring the new industrial wealth; rich supplies of the former were obtainable in the East Indies, and of the latter in Guinea and the Transvaal. Sugar cane and coffee, cocoa and tea, bananas and dates, if not directly serviceable to industrial machinery, were very palatable to the enlarging European multitude that tended it.

But commercial expansion into the tropics was a novelty of degree rather than of kind and hardly suffices to explain the political imperialism of the '70's and '80's. This was inaugurated prior to any general resort to tariff protectionism in Europe, and prior also to any universal export of capital.

Neither Russia nor Italy had surplus manufactures to dispose of or surplus wealth to invest; yet both engaged in the scramble for imperial dominion, the one with striking success and the other not. Germany exported little capital until after she had acquired an extensive colonial empire, and France secured a far more extensive one while her industrial development lagged behind Germany's. Great Britain had long had all the supposed economic motives for imperialism — export of manufactured goods, demand for raw materials, supply of surplus capital — and yet these did not move her in the '60's as much as they did in the '70's.[1] On the other hand, Norway, whose ocean-borne commerce was exceeded only by Great Britain's and Germany's, remained consistently aloof from overseas imperialism.

Apparently the flag of a European nation did not have to follow its trade — or its financial investments. But once flag raising became common and competitive in Africa and on the Pacific, economic considerations undoubtedly spurred most of the European participants to greater efforts and keener competition in those regions. Then the tariff protectionism of Continental nations was applied, in one form or another, to their respective colonies, and the more colonies each one had the greater were its opportunities for favorable trade and investment and the closer it approached to the ideal of all-around self-sufficiency. And to prevent too much of the world from being thus monopolized by France, Germany, Italy, or any other protectionist power, Great Britain moved mightily to gather the lion's share into her own free-trade empire. In other words, neo-mercantilism, once established, had very important imperialistic consequences.

The fact remains, nevertheless, that the founding of new colonial empires and the fortifying of old ones antedated the establishment of neo-mercantilism, and that the economic arguments adduced in support of imperialism seem to have been a rationalization *ex post facto*. In the main, it was not Liberal parties, with their super-abundance of industrialists and bankers, who sponsored the outward imperialistic thrusts of the '70's and early '80's. Instead, it was Conservative parties, with a preponderantly agricultural clientele notoriously suspicious of moneylenders and big business, and, above all, it was patriotic professors and publicists regardless of political affiliation and unmindful of personal economic interest. These put forth the economic arguments which eventually drew bankers and traders and industrialists into the imperialist camp.

Basically the new imperialism was a nationalistic phenomenon. It followed hard upon the national wars which created an all-powerful Germany and a united Italy, which carried Russia within sight of Constantinople, and which left England fearful and France eclipsed. It expressed a resulting psychological reaction, an ardent desire to maintain or recover national prestige. France sought compensation for European loss in oversea gain. England would offset her European isolation by enlarging and glorifying the British Empire. Russia, halted in the Balkans, would turn anew to Asia, and before long Germany and Italy would show the world that the prestige they had won by might inside Europe they were entitled to enhance by imperial exploits outside. The lesser powers, with no great prestige at stake, managed to get on without any new imperialism, though Portugal and Holland displayed a revived pride in the empires they already possessed and the latter's was administered with renewed vigor.

---

[1] It should be remarked, however, that the depression which began in 1873, by limiting opportunities for profitable investment in countries already largely industrialized, probably stimulated investment in "backward" regions and may thus have contributed to a revival of imperialistic interests and ambitions. Nevertheless, this was truer of Great Britain than of any nation on the Continent, and it scarcely suffices to explain why with almost all the great powers (and only with them) political imperialism preceded any substantial financial investment in particular regions appropriated. [Author's note]

Public agitation for extending overseas the political dominion of European national states certainly began with patriotic intellectuals. As early as 1867 Lothar Bucher, one of Bismarck's associates in the Prussian foreign office, published in the influential *Norddeutsche Allgemeine Zeitung* a series of articles endorsing and advertising the hitherto neglected counsels of Friedrich List: "Companies should be founded in the German seaports to buy lands in foreign countries and settle them with German colonies; also companies for commerce and navigation whose object would be to open new markets abroad for German manufacturers and to establish steamship lines. . . . Colonies are the best means of developing manufactures, export and import trade, and finally a respectable navy."

The next year Otto Kersten, traveler and explorer, founded at Berlin a "Central Society for Commercial Geography and German Interests Abroad," with an official journal, *Der Export*. Simultaneously the "Royal Colonial Institute" was founded at London; and a brilliant young English gentleman, Sir Charles Dilke, returning from a trip around the world, published his patriotic and immensely popular *Greater Britain*. Two years later, in the midst of the Franco-Prussian War, the redoubtable Froude scored his fellow Englishmen in the pages of *Fraser's Magazine* for their blindness to imperial glories. In 1872 Disraeli practically committed the Conservative party in Britain to a program of imperialism, and in 1874 Paul Leroy-Beaulieu, dean of political economists in France and implacable foe of tariff protection, plumped for French imperialism in a "scientific" treatise, *De la Colonisation chez les peuples modernes*.

These were foretastes. Heartier fare was served immediately after the Russo-Turkish War and the Congress of Berlin. In 1879 Friedrich Fabri, a pious promoter of Christian foreign missions, asked rhetorically "Does Germany need Colonies?" and answered with a resounding "Yes!" Germany's surplus population, he argued, should have

places where it could go and still buy German goods and share in the other blessings of German *Kultur*. Fabri was eloquently seconded in 1881 by Hübbe-Schleiden, a lawyer and sometime explorer in equatorial Africa, who now insisted that through imperialistic endeavors "a country exhibits before the world its strength or weakness as a nation." In like vein the historian Treitschke edified his student audiences at the University of Berlin with the moral that "every virile people has established colonial power."

In 1882 a frankly propagandist "Colonial Society" was formed in Germany through the joint efforts of a naturalist, a geographer, and a politician, while in France Professor Leroy-Beaulieu brought out a new edition of his classic with the dogmatic addendum that "colonization is for France a question of life and death: either France will become a great African power, or in a century or two she will be no more than a secondary European power; she will count for about as much in the world as Greece and Rumania in Europe." The following year Professor John Seeley published his celebrated Cambridge lectures on the *Expansion of England*. The book took the British public by storm. It sold 80,000 copies within a brief time and won for its author the warm discipleship of Lord Rosebery[2] and a knighthood.

In 1883 the stridently imperialistic "Primrose League" was launched by Tory Democrats, and soon afterwards the more sedate "Imperial Federation League" by nationalistic Liberals. In 1883, also, was founded a "Society for German Colonization." And capping the academic contributions to the imperialist cause, Froude published *Oceana* in 1885, while Alfred Rambaud, historian of Russia and first occupant of the chair in contemporary history at the Sorbonne, edited in 1886 a co-operative work on *La France coloniale*.

Already, statesmen were following the

[2] Rosebery was Liberal foreign secretary, 1886, 1892–94, and prime minister, 1894–95. [Editor's note]

professors and proclaiming that commerce and investments should follow the flag. If Gladstone hesitated, Disraeli and Salisbury did not; nor did such "new" Liberals as Rosebery, Chamberlain, and Grey. Jules Ferry surely did not hesitate. Replying to parliamentary critics of his aggressive policy in Tunis and Tonkin, he marshaled in speeches from 1881 to 1885 all the professorial arguments: that superior races have a civilizing mission to inferior races; that an industrial nation needs colonial markets; that coaling stations are requisite for navy and mercantile marine; and that if France refrained from imperialism, she would "descend from the first rank to the third or fourth." Bismarck seemed to hesitate more than he actually did. He privately expressed sympathy with imperialist ambitions in 1876 and publicly backed them, at least in the case of Samoa, in 1879. By 1884–85 he was persuading the Reichstag that colonies were vital to national economy. "Colonies would mean the winning of new markets for German industries, the expansion of trade, and a new field for German activity, civilization, and capital."

Most simply, the sequence of imperialism after 1870 appears to have been, first, pleas for colonies on the ground of national prestige; second, getting them; third, disarming critics by economic argument; and fourth, carrying this into effect and relating the results to the neo-mercantilism of tariff protection and social legislation at home.

There were, of course, complexities in the imperialistic movement. In so far as it was economic, it did not affect the "capitalist class" as a whole, but only particular business interests: exporters and manufacturers of certain commodities such as calico and cheap alcoholic beverages; importers of rubber, raw cotton, coffee, copra, etc.; shipping magnates; some bankers, though a very small percentage of all; and those "parasites of imperialism," the makers of arms and uniforms, the producers of telegraph and railway material, etc. But these last did not "cause" imperialism; they merely throve on it.

Christian missions provided an important adjunct to imperialism. They spread and multiplied in the second half of the nineteenth century as never before, in part as a reaction, we have suggested elsewhere, to the prevalent materialism in Europe, and in larger part because of the immensely improved means of travel and communication throughout the world. A missionary might have gone his way, like a merchant, the one conveying spiritual and the other material goods to heathen peoples, without any thought of raising a national flag over them or subjecting them to European rule. Actually, however, missionaries like merchants lived in a nationalistic age, and many of them were quite willing, on occasion, to invoke the naval or military protection of their respective national states. Not a few of Europe's footholds in other Continents were obtained as penalties for the persecution of Christian missionaries. Even where missionaries did not directly prompt the extension of European dominion, they frequently paved the way for adventurers who did; and stories published back home by them or about them stimulated popular interest in, and support of, imperial undertakings. About David Livingstone, for example, something like a cult grew up in England, so that when he died in the wilds of Africa on May Day, 1873, his body was borne with hierophantic solemnity all the way to Zanzibar and thence under naval escort to England, where finally it was deposited amid Britain's national heroes in Westminster Abbey on April 18, 1874. The year was that of Disraeli's accession to the premiership, and for the popular favor accorded his subsequent imperial activities, he should have thanked the dead Livingstone more than any live merchant or banker.

It was a time, too, when evolutionary biology was beginning to occupy a central place in European thought, when hundreds of naturalists, emulating Darwin, engaged in scientific expeditions to strange distant regions and furnished millions of ordinary stay-at-homes with fascinating descriptions of the extraordinary flora and fauna they had observed. Already in 1861 the Franco-American Du Chaillu had reported from Gabun in equatorial Africa his amazing discovery of the gorilla, which was readily imagined to be the "missing link" between ape and man. In 1867 he published an account of a race of pygmies he had found, and for years afterwards his pen poured out popular tales of African adventure. Meanwhile, in the early '70's, Faidherbe was exploring upper Egypt, Nachtigal was visiting Khartum, De Brazza was following Du Chaillu into the hinterland of Gabun, Skobelev with notebook in hand was investigating the borders of Turkestan, Evelyn Baring (the later Lord Cromer) was describing the natural wonders of India, and Henry Morton Stanley was "finding" Livingstone for the New York *Herald* and an avid public, and then heading an Anglo-American scientific expedition into the vast Congo basin. Presently George Goldie was exploring the Niger country, Joseph Thomson was leading an expedition into east-central Africa, Harry Johnston was traversing Angola and meeting Stanley on the Congo, and Frederick Lugard, a young veteran of the Afghan War, was penetrating Nyasaland and Uganda.

Of these explorers, the majority had military training. Faidherbe was a French general, former governor of Senegal, and Skobelev a Russian general who was to win laurels in the Russo-Turkish War. Nachtigal was a German army surgeon, De Brazza a French naval officer. Cromer and Goldie and Lugard had all been British soldiers. As a group they were intensely patriotic, and they nicely combined with scientific interests a zeal to serve the political, economic, and military interests of their respective nations. They were prime promoters of imperialism, and most of them remained as pro-consuls of provinces they charted and helped to appropriate.

Sheer love of adventure was a potent lure to imperialism. Africa in particular, by reason of the widespread advertising its marvels and dangers received at the beginning of the '70's, beckoned to bold and venturesome spirits in Europe, and some of the boldest became empire-builders in the grand style, in a few cases acquiring fabulous personal wealth, in all cases experiencing that sense of power which comes from great achievement. Stanley was patently an adventurer. He had no surplus goods to sell, no surplus capital to invest. He was a self-made man, if ever there was one. A Welshman by birth, with the original name of Rowlands, he ran away from home and school at an early age to find work in Liverpool, first in a haberdasher's shop, then with a butcher. When this grew tedious he worked his way across the Atlantic to New Orleans and fell in with a merchant by the name of Stanley, who adopted him. At the outbreak of the American Civil War he enlisted in the Confederate army, only to be taken prisoner at the battle of Shiloh; then, "with ready versatility he joined the Union army to fight against his former comrades-in-arms. Toward the close of the war he discovered a latent talent for journalism, which, when peace returned, led him to Salt Lake City to describe the extraordinary customs of the Mormons, then to Asia Minor in search of thrilling adventure, then with General Hancock against the Indians, with the British against Abyssinia, and to Crete, and Spain." He went to central Africa in 1871 because he was sent, but he remained to build a huge empire for another and the queerest kind of adventurer — a man who was not self-made and who never set foot in Africa, but who was as hypnotized by African dreams as by female realities — Leopold of the Belgians, Leopold of the Congo Free State.

But the adventurer-imperialist *par excellence* was Cecil Rhodes, and his extraordinary career began by accident. A sickly youth, son of an Anglican clergyman and intended for the church, he was bundled off in 1870, for purposes of health, to an elder brother's farm in southern Africa. He arrived just when diamonds were discovered in the near-by Kimberley fields. He joined other diggers, dug more industriously and successfully, and within a year found himself wealthy and healthy. He returned to England for study at Oxford, but the study was desultory and he was soon back permanently in South Africa, adding gold mines to diamond mines, running Cape politics, projecting British sway the entire length of the Continent up to Cairo, and doing much to realize it.

The star German adventurer was Carl Peters. Son of a Lutheran clergyman and graduate of the University of Berlin, he contracted imperialist fever on a visit to England and set out in 1884 in disguise and under an alias — he was still in his twenties — to build an empire in East Africa. His method was simple, and the results startling, even to Bismarck. By a judicious distribution of toys plus injudicious application of grog, he got twelve big black chieftains, within ten days, to make their X's on documents conveying to Germany a total of 60,000 square miles. But that was only a start. Peters kept right on enlarging German East Africa until an Anglo-German convention of 1890 set bounds to his activity.

Explorers and adventurers gave rise to a peculiar species of organizer and administrator, despotic and ruthless and most devotedly imperialistic. Peters and Rhodes were transmuted by the African environment into this species, and so too were Cromer in Egypt and Milner at the Cape. For the glory of themselves and their countries, such local potentates carried on without too much regard for merely economic considerations or for the international engagements of their distant home governments. They were on the spot and knew better than London or Berlin or any other capital what had to be done, and they usually did it in an expansive way.

The actual course of empire — the order in which distant areas were appropriated by European powers — was determined less by design than by chance. Murder of a missionary or trader and consequent forceful intervention might occur anywhere. In some instances, curiously frequent in Moslem countries, native rulers practically invited intervention by living far beyond their means and contracting debts which they were unable to repay. Such was the basis of European imperialism in Egypt, Tunis, Persia, and to a large extent in Turkey. For example, the Khedive Ismail of Egypt, a squat, red-bearded gentleman with a passion for ostentation and the externals of European culture, spent half a billion dollars in the twelve years after his accession in 1863, running up the Egyptian public debt from 16 million to 342 million and continuing to borrow money from European bankers at ever more onerous rates. In 1875 he could only get a quarter of the face value of short-term bonds bearing 20 per cent interest. In 1876 he sold his shares of Suez Canal Company stock to England, and consented to joint supervision of his finances by representatives of England, France, Italy, and Austria. Soon this control was narrowed to England and France, and in 1882 to England alone. No doubt bankers and investors egged on both the khedive to spend and the English government to collect, but a less prodigal khedive, and one more intelligently concerned with the welfare of his subjects, might have staved off foreign rule. The contemporary Mikado of Japan did.

Especially active in directing the course of empire after 1870 were the European colonists already settled in Algeria, South Africa, and Australasia. These performed the same function in the latter part of the nineteenth century as their prototypes in the America of the eighteenth century. French settlers in Algeria were more eager than the government at Paris to make all adjacent African lands French. British and Dutch settlers in South Africa had almost a psychosis about others getting anywhere near them, and from the former, rather than from London, came the main drive for British expansion northward. Australians and New Zealanders were continually pressing the home government to forestall alien seizure of South Sea islands.

In many instances European flags were hoisted as a sport — a competitive sport — with about the same indifference to economic motives as characterized the later planting of American and other flags on cakes of ice around the North or South Pole. As one reads of successive French flag raisings in oases of the Sahara and on coral reefs of the Pacific, one gets a lively impression that it was all *pour le sport*.

Some capitalists undoubtedly promoted imperialism, and more profited by it. But in the last analysis it was the nationalistic masses who made it possible and who most vociferously applauded and most constantly backed it. Disraeli and Joseph Chamberlain were good politicians as well as patriots, and with a clairvoyance greater than Gladstone's, they perceived that in a country where the masses were patriotic, literate, and in possession of the ballot, a political party which frankly espoused imperialism would have magnetic attraction for them. So it proved. An unwonted popularity attended the Conservative parties of Britain and Germany during the '80's and '90's. The masses, of course, had no immediate economic interest in the matter, and it would have required an extraordinary act of faith on their part to believe the predictions of imperialistic intellectuals that somehow, sometime, everybody would be enriched from the Congo or the Niger or Tahiti. Rather, the masses were thrilled and stirred by front-page news in the popular press of far-off things and battles still to come. They devoured the yarns of a Rider Haggard — he had been secretary to the governor of Natal in the '70's and he

knew his Africa. They learned by heart the vulgar verses of a Rudyard Kipling — he had lived in India and been a chum of doughty, swearing British soldiers. And the sporting impulse which drew crowds to prize fights and to football and cricket matches, evoked a whole nation's lusty cheers for its "team" in the mammoth competitive game of imperialism.

Into the imperial-mindedness of the masses, scarcely less than into that of Rhodes or Peters, Ferry or Chamberlain, fitted neatly the preaching of Darwinian sociology, that human progress depends upon struggle between races and nations and survival of the fittest. Obviously most eligible for the "fittest" were the white peoples of Europe, who therefore owed it to science as well as to civilization (and religion) to establish their supremacy over inferior populations in all other continents. Which of them would ultimately be adjudged the absolutely fittest would depend on the outcome of conflict among themselves as well as with lesser breeds. This preaching justified competitive imperialism and cloaked attendant ruthlessness in the mantle of idealistic devotion to duty. It was summarized by Kipling at the close of the generation (1899) in his famous lines:

> Take up the White Man's Burden —
>   Send forth the best ye breed —
> Go bind your sons to exile
>   To serve your captives' need;
> To wait in heavy harness,
>   On fluttered fold and wild —
> Your new-caught, sullen peoples,
>   Half-devil and half-child.

DIPLOMATIC REASONS FOR EXPANSION

NICHOLAS MANSERGH

Nicholas Mansergh (1910–   ) is currently Smuts Professor of the History of the British Commonwealth and a fellow of St. John's College, Cambridge. He is the author of many books, particularly on Ireland and on British Commonwealth affairs. *The Coming of the First World War,* based on a series of lectures given in 1944, is a reinterpretative essay on the pre-World War I period in general. International relations are at the core of Mansergh's historical commentary and of his discussion of European expansion.

THE opening up of Africa was the work not of governments but of individuals possessed of great courage and remarkable powers of endurance. There is something very revealing in that description by a companion, of Livingstone "tramping along with the steady, heavy tread which kept one in mind that he had walked across Africa." But where individuals had pioneered, governments soon intervened, and it is only with the motives that prompted their intervention that this book is concerned. The political and economic importance of Africa was popularly overestimated. In Western Europe it was commonly believed that the acquisition of colonies was the high road to rapid economic development. Many writers, principally, though not only, German, failed, as Mr. Taylor has written, "to grasp the truth about the British Empire — that it had come into being as the result of British commercial enterprise and industrial success; and they asserted the reverse, that the prosperity and wealth of Great Britain were due to the existence of her Empire. The German campaign for colonies rested on the simple dogma — give Germany colonies and the Germans will then be as prosperous as the English."[1] Such popular beliefs may have influenced the minds even of autocratic governments, but they were not the directing force in overseas colonial expansion. The rulers of Europe thought primarily in terms of political not economic advantage and it was on the struggle for power in Europe that their eyes were always fixed. Expansion overseas was for the Continental States, not an end, but a means to an end.

Bismarck was a late and always a sceptical convert to "colonialism." His indifference was a source of strength. In the colonial field he could play the hand that best suited his purpose in Europe. For it was on the European scene that his eye was always riveted. And not his alone. "If you were to bring me all the empires of Asia and Africa . . . ," said General Garnier des Garets, "they wouldn't in my eyes be worth an acre of the earth where I fought in 1870, and where the *Cuirassiers* of Reichshoffen and the Zouaves of Froeschwiller lie." But the balance of forces in Europe left France after 1870 with the alternatives of enlarging her Empire overseas or a policy

[1] A. J. P. Taylor: *Germany's First Bid for Colonies 1884–5,* London, 1938, p. 4. [Author's note]

From Nicholas Mansergh, *The Coming of the First World War. A Study in the European Balance, 1878–1914* (London, 1949), pp. 43–45, 46–52, 56–58, 61–62; Copyright 1949. By permission of Longmans, Green and Co. Ltd.

of resignation. Alsace-Lorraine could only be a question "reserved for the future." In the meantime, was it not folly to sit by idly nursing wrongs while other Powers extended their control over large parts of Africa and Asia? "Au nom d'un chauvinisme exalté et à courtes vues," exclaimed Jules Ferry, the protagonist of Republican imperialism, "devrions-nous acculer la politique française dans une impasse et, les yeux fixés sur la ligne bleue des Vosges, laisser tout faire, tout s'engager, tout se résoudre, sans nous, autour de nous, contre nous?"[2] This was the reasoning produced by the psychological reaction to defeat and reinforced by a revival of France's traditional belief in mercantilist economics that led her, a country with a declining population, to embark, with direct encouragement from Bismarck, on an active policy of colonial expansion in North and Central Africa, in Madagascar and in Indo-China.

Bismarck's sympathetic interest in French imperialism was an experiment on his side, in the possibilities of Franco-German reconciliation. That France should remain ostracized in Europe was his settled policy, but clearly it was not in the interests of Germany that she should be driven to despair. An outlet for her energies, preoccupation in colonial fields in which Germany had no interest, except for bargaining purposes, had everything to recommend it. The fact that, incidentally, French expansion in North Africa, and particularly in Tunis, would bring her into conflict with Italy, enhanced the attractions of this policy, even if it were not its primary purpose. To the French Ambassador, in January 1879, the Chancellor gave effusive encouragement. "Now indeed, I believe," observed Bismarck, "that the Tunisian pear is ripe and that the time has come for you to pluck it. The effrontery of the Bey has

been like the August sun for this African fruit, which might very well have been spoilt or stolen by somebody else if you had let it remain too long on the bough. I don't know what you intend to do or whether it tempts you, but I take the opportunity of repeating . . . my desire to give you proofs of my good will on questions which concern you and in which there are no German interests in opposition to yours." That Italy had already received German encouragement to seize Tunis must have heightened the Chancellor's satisfaction with French reactions. For his advice was heeded, and by the end of 1881 this former province of the Turkish Empire was securely French and Italy estranged.

Not only France and Italy but also England had traditional interests in North Africa. If it was the anxiety of the Third Republic to restore French self-respect after 1870; of a united Italy to raise herself to the level of a first-class Power by the acquisition of colonies on the southern shore of the Mediterranean; it was England's concern for imperial communications that led her with some reluctance to intervene in Egypt and so come into conflict with France. The Suez Canal of which control had been dramatically acquired by Disraeli was, as Bismarck admitted, "of vital importance" to her Empire, being "like the spinal cord which connects the backbone with the brain." It was that fact that left England no freedom of choice. After "Dual Control" had been established in Egypt in the interests of British and French bond-holders in 1876, Lord Salisbury summed up the alternatives before his country. "You may," he said, "renounce, or monopolize or share. Renouncing would have been to place France across our road to India. Monopolizing would have been very near the risk of war. So we resolved to share.". . .

England's task in Egypt was undertaken with German goodwill, which soon evaporated. Where Bismarck had once acknowledged comparative German indifference in the affairs of Egypt, he felt by the end of 1883 that the time had come when a less

2 "Must we, in the name of an excessive and short-sighted chauvinism, drive French policy into an impasse and, with our eyes fixed on the blue line of the Vosges, let everything be done, everything be undertaken, everything be decided — without us, around us, against us?" [Editor's note]

passive attitude would better serve his ends. "We are uncommonly grateful to Prince Bismarck," Lord Granville had said to Count Herbert Bismarck in January 1883, "for the friendly attitude of German policy this summer was of great service to us. Our being left with a free hand in Egypt we owe, when all is said, to Germany's goodwill. We are all aware that at a particular moment Prince Bismarck could have upset the coach if he had chosen to, and we realize with much thankfulness that he refrained from doing so." The price however had still to be paid, and in Egypt pressure was easy to apply. For the Gladstone Government, reluctant to contemplate annexation on principle, were left with no practicable alternative to acting as the nominal mandatory of the Powers. That left Britain in a weak and vulnerable position, for, of the Powers, France burned with resentment at her exclusion from Egypt, and Russia, without any direct interest in the Nile Valley, was hostile to the consolidation of Britain's position in the Eastern Mediterranean. This was a situation from which Bismarck was not slow to profit. The situation in Egypt made England, as Baring[3] frankly recognized, dependent on German goodwill.

It seems clear now that Bismarck's colonial policy was more the incidental offshoot of tactical moves in Europe than a departure undertaken on its own merits. The price that Bismarck was most concerned to exact from England in return for German goodwill in Egypt, was some form of guarantee in Europe which would reinsure Germany in the West against French aggression. When it was made plain that this was a price that England was not prepared to pay he decided to explore again the possibility of friendship with France, founded on Franco-German hostility to England in the colonial field. That he was also influenced by internal political considerations is hardly to be denied. A forward colonial

[3] Sir Evelyn Baring, later first Earl of Cromer, was British agent and consul general in Egypt from 1883 to 1907. [Editor's note]

policy was well calculated to enhance the Chancellor's popularity at home.

While early in 1884 the German Ambassador in London, Count Münster, was happily contemplating the friendly acquisition of Heligoland, encouraged at once by the Chancellor's interest, and the remark of the Colonial Secretary, Lord Derby, who said "this perfectly useless piece of rock in the North Sea, the smallest of our Colonies, gives me the most trouble of any," a far-ranging area of Anglo-German colonial friction loomed on the horizon. The Chancellor took up the grievances of German traders in Fiji; he then turned a more formidable gaze on South-West Africa. The Ambassador was instructed "to cease to mention the question of Heligoland" because it might make German colonial claims seem of secondary importance. If Germany failed to obtain satisfaction for her claims overseas, the Chancellor declared that "she must try to gain closer touch with seafaring Powers, France included." But in actual fact the colonial grievances had been put forward largely because they might make closer co-operation with France possible. It was on the foundation of joint hostility to Great Britain overseas that Bismarck hoped to build up friendship with France.

From 1883 to 1885 the new policy was put into practice. The weak but well-meaning Foreign Secretary, Lord Granville, noticed with dismay the abrupt change in the temper of Anglo-German relations. An atmosphere of friendly co-operation was transformed by a recital of German grievances in many parts of the world, which lost nothing in the telling by the Chancellor's arrogant son, Count Herbert Bismarck. Of all the disputes which followed, the most protracted was concerned with the fate of Angra Pequeña on the west coast of Africa some 200 miles north of the frontier of the Cape Province. There a German trader, named Lüderitz, established himself and asked for protection. Could the British Government give protection? inquired Herbert Bismarck, for "if not, the German

Government will do their best to extend to it the same measure of protection which they could give to their subjects in remote parts of the world — but without having the least desire to establish any footing in South Africa." In replying to his inquiry there was unpardonable delay due partly, as Lord Granville explained, to the need of consulting the Cape. "We cannot," he observed, "act except in agreement with the Government of the Colony which has an independent Ministry and Parliament." To Bismarck this sounded singularly unconvincing. But there was a difference of view between London and the Cape. To a German settlement in South-West Africa, London might be comparatively indifferent, but the Cape was resolutely opposed. And in the event, what began as an inquiry about protection at Angra Pequeña developed, against their wishes, into German South-West Africa. The reasons are to be found in the weakness of the British position in Egypt, which made dependence on German goodwill inevitable, and strained relations with Russia which made the more desirable friendly co-operation with the Triple Alliance.

By the end of 1855 Bismarck's new policy had laid the foundation of the German Colonial Empire, for by then she had secured her position in the Cameroons and in New Guinea as well as in South-West Africa together with a foothold in East Africa. Where the British Colonial Empire had been founded largely by the private enterprise of the chartered companies, Germany's was created through the impetus of a deliberate policy of state. If that policy met a weak and dilatory response in London, that was due to misunderstanding of its aim and not to unfriendliness. For it was generally accepted that it was right and just that Germany should have her "place in the Sun." Owing to earlier indifference and her late start, her African territories compared unfavourably with those of France or of the Belgians in the Congo Basin, or of the British. But, judged by her subsequent policy, her interest in

colonial expansion remained very secondary to her interests in Europe. By 1914 the total number of German colonial settlers was no more than 23,000. While the number of European emigrants is in itself no criterion of the quality of colonial government, these trifling numbers are at least an indication that colonies did not serve as an outlet for surplus population in Germany.

While Germany was acquiring a Colonial Empire in Africa and the Pacific, France, assured of German goodwill, extended her empire chiefly in North and West Africa but also by the acquisition of Madagascar, a convenient stepping-stone to Indo-China, between 1883 and 1885, and after a protracted struggle in Tonkin and Annam. It was the losses and set-backs in Tonkin that brought about the fall of the second Ferry Ministry, and with it the end of an active imperialist policy leaning on German goodwill. "The patronage of Bismarck," noted Lord Lyons, British Ambassador in Paris, "overthrew the Freycinet Cabinet; it is not strengthening Jules Ferry. . . . The *revanche* is still at the bottom of every French heart." With the fall of Ferry, that was no longer to be disguised. Bismarck's colonial policy, in so far as it was an experiment in Franco-German reconciliation, had failed.

The years 1885–89 witnessed the height of the scramble for Africa. But unlike the preceding years they were marked by a revival of Anglo-German co-operation under the aegis of Bismarck and Salisbury. If Bismarck, in laying the foundations of a German Colonial Empire, had not effected a reconciliation with France, he had at least succeeded in his other objectives. France and Italy were estranged over Tunis and Italy was compelled to seek alliance with the Central Powers: England and France were divided by Egypt; and England, partly because of her concern for the security of the Nile Valley, which was the cardinal consideration in determining her colonial policy in Africa, and partly because of the advance of Russia to the Afghan frontier, was also impelled towards more friendly relations with the Central Powers. This had two consequences. The first was the Mediterranean Agreement of 1887 by which England reached an understanding, first with Italy, later extended to Austria, to preserve the *status quo* in the Mediterranean. Highly satisfying to Bismarck, under whose auspices it was negotiated, the agreement brought England, even if loosely, into the orbit of the Triple Alliance Powers. The other consequence was to be found in the general Anglo-German colonial settlement in Africa, concluded in 1890 after Bismarck's fall, and made possible by the cession of Heligoland. In the first instance it was hoped by the Germans that South-West Africa might be surrendered for Heligoland. Count Herbert Bismarck, very unfavourably impressed by a visit to South-West Africa, sponsored this proposal. "I think," he wrote on 27th March 1889, "the deal would be very advantageous to us and enormously popular in Germany. Our South-West African Company is stagnant, bankrupt and hopeless. . . . In the colonial area we have not in fact a single soul who would qualify as a German citizen." But the negotiations proceeded slowly, largely because Bismarck was once more concerned with the possibility of negotiating a wider agreement with England which would carry European commitments, and partly because he felt it was the course of prudence to go slow lest it might be suspected in London how much importance Germany attached to an island which commanded the entrance to the Kiel Canal, then being built. When agreement was finally reached, the *quid pro quo* for England was not in South-West but mainly in East Africa. The Sultanate of Zanzibar became a British Protectorate and German penetration in East Africa was barred by the delineation of the boundaries of British East Africa.

RUSSIAN EXPANSION IN ASIA

If German support for French imperial ambitions was an experiment which was tried, failed and abandoned, there was a remarkable consistency about Germany's attitude to Russian expansion in Asia. It was something to be encouraged. About that there were no doubts. It had almost everything to recommend it. It would distract Russia's attention from Europe, thereby lessening the risk of an Austro-Russian conflict in the Balkans; it would keep Russian forces harmlessly occupied; it would, above all, keep alive Anglo-Russian tension by playing on English fears of a Russian invasion of India. "Germany," Bismarck advised his Emperor, "has no interest in preventing Russia if she looks for the occupation which is necessary for her army in Asia rather than in Europe. If the Russian Army is unoccupied it becomes a danger to the internal security of the Empire and the dynasty, and if occupation fails in Asia it must necessarily be sought on the Western front. . . . It is therefore an aim of German policy to-day to bring about hostile rather than too intimate relations between Russia and England." With the Penjdeh incident in 1885, hostility nearly brought the two countries to war, much to Germany's satisfaction, before a settlement of the Afghan frontier was reached. In more flamboyant language and by more direct methods the Kaiser Wilhelm II pursued, in this respect at least, the same policies as the Chancellor he had deposed from office. "Clearly," he wrote to the Tsar Nicholas II in April 1895, "it is the great task of the future for Russia to cultivate the Asian continent and to defend Europa from the inroads of the great Yellow Race. In this you will always find me ready to help you as best I can. You have well understood the call of Providence. . . ." But though German policy was consistent, Russia, unlike France, was not a defeated country and her expansion in Central Asia owed little or nothing to German encouragement or German goodwill. Like the British in India, the frontiers of the Russian Empire in Central Asia moved steadily forward because the vacuum in power that existed in the Trans-Caspian regions left her with little alternative. . . .

THE JAMESON RAID AND THE SOUTH AFRICAN WAR

It was Lord Salisbury who remarked that Gladstone's impassioned fight for Irish Home Rule had aroused the slumbering genius of Imperialism. It is doubtful, however, if the blatant and boastful temper of the *fin de siècle* deserves so kindly a description. One of its most notable consequences was to estrange Britain from Europe at a moment when her isolation placed her in a position whose perils were better understood in retrospect than at the time.

It was in January 1895 that President Kruger,[4] as the guest of the German Club in Pretoria on the Kaiser's birthday, spoke of Germany as "a grown-up power that would stop England from kicking the child Republic." On instructions from London the British Ambassador protested against the German encouragement of Boer hostility to Britain, of which Kruger's speech was regarded as a provocative expression. The Kaiser later maintained that the Ambassador had gone so far as to mention the "astounding word, 'war'." "For a few square miles full of niggers and palm trees England had threatened her one true friend, the German Emperor, grandson of Her Majesty the Queen of Great Britain and Ireland, with war!" According to his own highly coloured narrative the Kaiser retorted with the "clear warning" that England could only escape from her existing isolation "by a frank and outspoken attitude either for or against the Triple Alliance." As things were England's attitude, her policy "of selfishness and bullying" were forcing Germany to make "common cause with France and Russia, each of whom had about a million men ready to pour in over my frontier. . . ." Into this atmosphere of artificial tension came with explosive effect the news of the Jameson Raid. Ill-judged, ill-considered, wholly indefensible, even in its limited Anglo-South African context, it

played straight into the hands of the most dangerous forces at work in Germany. The Kaiser responded with a telegram to President Kruger, dated 3rd January 1896. "I express my sincere congratulations that, supported by your people, without appealing for the help of friendly Powers, you have succeeded by your own energetic action against armed bands which invaded your country as disturbers of the peace, and have thus been enabled to restore peace and safeguard the independence of the country against attacks from the outside." If the telegram was designed to embody every phrase best calculated to inflame sentiment in a country whose first reaction to the news of the Raid was one of profound misgiving, it could not have been better drafted. At once opinion hardened against the Boer Republics. President Kruger was no longer felt to be the much wronged defender of his people's rights, but a collaborator with the Kaiser challenging British rule in South Africa. Self-respect was restored and internal divisions papered over.

To send a telegram was one thing; to intervene effectively in South Africa was another. Germany had no fleet. What course was open to her? Holstein[5] supplied the answer. The Triple Alliance and the Dual Alliance should forget their rivalry and co-operate against Britain. There was a wide field for common action and many colonial ambitions that could be achieved in concert. France should receive the Congo Free State, Germany further concessions in China, Russia, Korea; Italy would become the Protector of Abyssinia. This superficially was a tempting prospect for one and all. But behind it there were subtle reservations, soon suspected. The ultimate German intention was not the final estrangement of Britain but a practical demonstration of the dangers of isolation and of the need to co-operate with the Triple Alliance. That was why there was

---

[4] Paul Kruger was president of the Transvaal from 1883 to 1900. [Editor's note]

[5] Baron von Holstein: German diplomat and statesman. [Editor's note]

no mention of Egypt. In the sequel it was in Paris that this grandiose plan received its death sentence. It was Egypt alone by which France might have been momentarily deluded into a dangerous partnership and Egypt was not on offer. Moreover, the immediate background to this continental League lay in the Transvaal, and the Transvaal was of no interest to France, however much its people might sympathize with the Boer cause. There must be, commented *Le Temps,* "no unnatural alliance" arising out of Anglo-German disputes in South Africa.

Holstein's project of European Alliance was stillborn, and it is interesting to notice that when the South African War broke out in 1899, Germany's policy was very different. In 1900 it was Russia who proposed mediation and Germany who declined it, the Kaiser improving the occasion by informing the Queen and the Prince of Wales of his refusal. The Prince paid ironic tribute to this gesture thanking the Kaiser in March 1900 — "You have no idea, my dear William, how all of us in England appreciate the loyal friendship you manifest towards us on every occasion." But if the political response was more judicious

the lesson deduced in Berlin from the Raid and the South African War was always the same — sea power is the condition of world power. That was the most significant legacy of the Jameson Raid and the South African War to Europe. . . .

THE LEGACY OF IMPERIAL EXPANSION

Though on more than one occasion colonial rivalries brought the Great Powers within sight of war, it is not for that reason to be concluded that colonial rivalry was a fundamental cause of war. On the contrary the colonial policies of the Continental states were formulated in the light of the European balance of power and designed to serve European ends. When they no longer served those ends the colonial scene slips unobtrusively into the background. From 1900 onwards there were no important colonial disputes between Germany and England because of the preoccupation of the Powers in the Far East between 1900–1904; and after 1904 because the Anglo-French Entente had removed the possibility of attaining the political ends which German colonial policy in the 'eighties had been designed to promote. . . .

THE POLITICS OF IMPERIALIST EXPANSION

PIERRE RENOUVIN

> The distinguished French historian, Pierre Renouvin (1893–   ),
> who among other positions holds those of Professor of contemporary
> history and Dean of the Faculty of Letters at the Sorbonne, has written
> with particular authority on the late nineteenth and early twentieth cen-
> turies. The introduction to *Les Politiques d'expansion impérialiste*, ex-
> cerpted below, attempts to generalize about the common elements in
> the policies and motivations of Jules Ferry of France, Joseph Chamber-
> lain of Britain, Leopold II of Belgium, Francesco Crispi[1] of Italy, and
> Theodore Roosevelt of the United States. Although it does not pretend
> to rest on extensive research, it does suggest the kinds of questions one
> must ask about the leading statesmen of the time.

I

"I n the realm of colonial history," said the introduction to the first volume of this series, "biographical study is always essential." Compared to the leaders who actually carried out the work, the statesmen who conceived it and who directed the policies of their countries in the new paths undoubtedly appear, in historical perspective, in lesser relief: they did not know the exaltation of the conqueror; they did not have the joy of forging an empire with their own hands or of doing as they chose each day. Without their impetus, however, would the work of expansion have been accomplished? Yes, perhaps. But it would have been under very different conditions. Certainly the economic and financial circumstances which dominated the life of the world led industrial states to extend their influence over "new countries" at the end of the nineteenth century, and the pressure of national sentiment favored imperialistic designs.

The statesman does not create out of nothing: he only knows how to recognize the possibilities which are open to him. But it is he who puts them to use. The "partition of the world" would not have been effected with the same rapidity if, in the majority of states qualified to conduct a policy of expansion, there had not been men who almost simultaneously made the same effort toward projecting their countries into the conquest of colonies or "spheres of influence." They could not always admit to their designs because they had to reckon with all the obstacles of internal politics and all the difficulties of foreign policy. Often their persistent line of action could not be disclosed in broad daylight. But if they had not been there to make the decisions, assume the responsibilities, weigh the risks, furnish the means of action, protect the "rear" of the enterprise by diplomatic action, would the movement of expansion have been the same? . . .

II

In pushing their countries into a policy of expansion, these statesmen were respond-

[1] In both his ministries as premier, 1887–91 and 1893–96, Crispi pursued an aggressive colonial policy. [Editor's note]

From Pierre Renouvin, "Introduction," in *Les Politiques d'expansion impérialiste* (*Colonies et empires*, vol. 5), Paris, 1949, pp. 1–2, 2–6, 7–8. By permission of Presses Universitaires de France. [Editor's translation]

ing to the same appeal: what they hoped to accomplish was to satisfy the needs of economic life, to assure the possession of naval bases and ports, to increase the prestige of the state. Economic necessities were stressed by each of them. Joseph Chamberlain was certainly convinced in this matter, because the difficulties which English exports ran up against were undeniable. Jules Ferry, when he invoked the necessity of finding markets for industrial products, doubtless did not have motives as pressing; and still less did Theodore Roosevelt, since American industry was only commencing at this time to feel the need to export. Yet Crispi, too, gave the same argument — to be sure, without insisting on it.

To English minds strategic exigencies were always present: was not the control of sea-lanes one of the essential elements of their power? And then, at the appeal of Alfred Mahan, the United States discovered the importance of naval bases, the possession of which became one of the aims — perhaps the essential aim — of American imperialism. Jules Ferry also used this argument in his great speech of July 28, 1885: he wanted to assure the navy of centers of supply for coal. "It is for that that we need Tunisia; that we need Saigon and Cochin China; that we need Madagascar." Crispi, although Italy was still not in a position, financially, to support an appreciable naval force, wanted to establish an Italian base at the entrance of the Red Sea, where England held Aden and France, Djibouti.

The moral obligations which the protection of national prestige imposed were invoked with even more insistence. "The British race," said Joseph Chamberlain, "is the greatest of governing races the world has ever seen." To maintain the "greatness" of the Empire, it was necessary to enlarge it, because the "unoccupied" countries, if they did not become English, would fall into the hands of other nations. Ferry echoed him: France, if she gave up exerting her influence outside of Europe, would abdicate her status as a great power, because Italy would be in Tunisia, England

in Madagascar or Tonkin. And the desire to increase the role of the United States in the world was expressed in 1898 by the group of American "imperialists." This parallel is striking: in London, in Washington, in Paris, and in Rome, the necessity of a policy of expansion was asserted in almost the same terms. And the analogy will be no less clear if one examines the *Weltpolitik* of William II.

Must one, however, let it go at that? Is one to believe that the action of these statesmen was determined solely by the necessities they pleaded? Must one see their imperialist doctrines as solely the result of their reasoning? Certainly not. They were all, or nearly all, driven into action by their own temperaments. At bottom, this was the determining moving force. In the case of Leopold II there is no doubt: that "prince of the Italian Renaissance" had a passion for power. Since he could not satisfy it in his tiny state, where his authority as constitutional monarch was too limited, he looked to Africa for a sphere of action proportionate to his desires. Theodore Roosevelt, throughout his life, was continually preaching and practicing "the strenuous life"; a man of letters — almost an historian — he glorified in his books the epic of the American pioneers and the heroism of the "white man." He retired from his presidency, at fifty years of age, to hunt big game and to explore the Brazilian jungle. Crispi had been involved in the Mazzinian struggles in his youth. Doubtless the behavior of a Joseph Chamberlain or a Jules Ferry was rather different: neither was, instinctively, an "imperialist," before he came to power. But apparently their "conversions" were dictated by deep propensities of their being, by sentiment even more than by reason. If Chamberlain became the advocate of expansion after having opposed the Egyptian adventure, was it not because he discerned a field of action where he could assert his capabilities as a statesman? And if Ferry, who before 1870 had not appeared to care about the colonial problem, and who, until his first ministry, had not manifested any particular interest in a program of expansion, became the founder of the new French Empire, was it not precisely because he looked, like Gambetta, for some compensation for the defeat of 1870? A policy of "withdrawal," he said, would be the "high road to decadence." Because France was still not up to resuming the role in continental politics which had been hers, it was necessary that she find a lofty goal to pursue outside of Europe. It was patriotic ardor, much more than the conviction of economic necessity, which led him toward imperialism.

III

Were these statesmen clearly conscious at the outset of the work they were being called on to fulfill? Did they choose the directions in which, when all is said and done, they led the expansion? Did they foresee the measures it would require? In short, did they have a plan? It is often possible to doubt this.

Leopold II, who when he was prince of Brabant had already been won over to the colonial idea and who unquestionably had an "imperial" goal from the beginning of his reign, knew where he was going, but not how to get there. It was only little by little that he discovered the means of realization. Crispi, before launching Italy on the Ethiopian adventure, had been opposed to it. If he suddenly perceived the importance of the Red Sea, it was only because he found out that expansion in the Mediterranean was no longer possible: Italy had lost Tunisia; she had run up against positions already taken in Egypt and even in Morocco; she could no longer think seriously at that time of Tripolitania, because the English government discouraged her. Crispi went to Ethiopia seeking a distraction from these disappointments. He claimed, it is true, that in the Red Sea Italy would be able to find the "key" to the Mediterranean. But did he really believe it? He wanted above all to make use of circumstances "to assert the name of Italy

in African regions," to show what a "great nation" was capable of — and originally had no other program than the preservation of "national honor."

Did there exist in Roosevelt's mind at the moment when he took the lead of the imperialist movement a clear idea of the goals to be reached? Had he traced in advance the broad lines of expansion in the Pacific or in Central America? Nothing like this appears in his writings or in his speeches. He had only the desire to profit from all favorable occasions which might present themselves — and he was the man to do it. He was the first to see the possibilities which the Spanish-American conflict was going to open with respect to the Philippines. He knew how to utilize the crisis in Colombia at the opportune moment in order to revive the old project of the Panama Canal. But it was only gradually, in relation to circumstances, that he established his plan of action.

Must one attribute a coordinated plan at least to Jules Ferry? He expounded such a plan, certainly, but after his fall. Admittedly, in revealing it earlier he would have committed a political indiscretion. Considering the opposition colonial action encountered, in public opinion as well as in the legislative chambers, he would have increased the difficulties of his task if he had announced his plans. But did he really have as early as 1880 the program he described in 1885? Did he have the desire to take France into Tunisia and Tonkin? It has not been proved; and the possibilities indicated by M. Julien[2] are indeed calculated to raise doubt. When in January and February, 1881, the French Council of Ministers on two occasions set aside the idea of an intervention in Tunisia, Jules Ferry, so far as the evidence permits us to follow his behavior, remained quiet. He did not decide to act until *after* the conversion of Gambetta. Nor did he, during his first ministry, have any particular inter-

[2] M. Julien wrote the article on Ferry in *Les Politiques d'expansion impérialiste.* [Editor's note]

est in the Tonkin situation, although all the terms of the question which he would know how to answer four years later were already specified. When he started out in this policy did he know where his steps would lead him? No, says M. Julien: he "let the events be his guide." This theory will not fail to provoke some surprise. Nevertheless, the case rests on very strong grounds. We still do not know, it is true, if there are documents in the private papers of Jules Ferry which would rectify this judgment.

The case of Joseph Chamberlain is simpler. In the great affairs with which he dealt — the Niger, the Upper Nile, and South Africa — he did not have to do the work of an initiator, because the broad lines of British policy in these regions had been fixed before his arrival in the colonial ministry, even before his "rallying" to the imperialist cause. It is very true that he gave a new character to this policy, more systematic and more ruthless; but he only innovated in methods and means. His personal contribution to the imperial program was of another sort: he wanted to organize the Empire, to establish a preferential system for commercial exchanges among the mother country, the Dominions, and the colonies. In this, only, was he an innovator: but it was in this, also, that he would meet with failure — all in opening a path to which Great Britain would return very much later.

Must one not then conclude that, everywhere, the policies of the imperialist statesmen were much more an adaptation to circumstances than the result of a deliberate plan? To acknowledge this is not to diminish their role.

IV

The great merit of these men lay not only in having understood how they could make use of circumstances and in having known immediately how to find the means of action. It was also and above all in having surmounted the obstacles which could check their moves: obstacles of foreign policy, which diplomacy had to try to re-move or circumvent; obstacles of internal politics, which, at least in France and Italy, were not the most negligible. . . .

Only Leopold II was able to ignore these parliamentary difficulties, at least at the time he created his Congo state. From being the president of an exploration society he became, in a few years, with astonishing craftiness and an exceptional talent for equivocal behavior, absolute ruler of a great territory in central Africa. He established an empire which was his personal handiwork without Belgium having anything to do with it. His colonial policy did not therefore depend on the Belgian parliament, and for fifteen years — until the time when financial difficulties would oblige him to ask the Belgian government for assistance — he was able to guide it with complete freedom. It was a unique opportunity.

Jules Ferry and Crispi, on the contrary, continually met with resistance in parliamentary circles which reflected the state of public opinion. Crispi had great difficulty in winning over the deputies in order to obtain the military forces and the necessary financial credits for the Ethiopian undertaking. Parliament's reluctance did not stop him: he acted when necessary outside of the legislative chambers. But he could not give the military leaders all the means which would insure their success. The attitude of the deputies was all the more reserved inasmuch as public opinion was hostile to the adventure. It was because Crispi took account neither of public opinion nor of the possibilities that he wound up with the disaster of Adowa. Jules Ferry succeeded because he had, with the same tenacity as Crispi, more clearsightedness and more authority. But his colonial policy was rudely disavowed by the legislative chamber — which did not however dare to wipe out its results. How can one explain this persistent hostility which finally reached a rare degree of violence, just after the failure of Lang-Son?[3] M. Julien's study

[3] Lang-Son: site of a Chinese victory over the French in Indochina, in 1885.

gives, with the rather strong frankness characteristic of historians, a suggestive and interesting interpretation which will not fail to excite debate. Jules Ferry, he says, could not count with confidence on the support of the majority of Parliament and of public opinion for his colonial policy, because it did not agree with the "bourgeois" spirit, the "market-garden" spirit (to use Keyserling's word) of the French people. Therefore he did not frankly explain his designs, and he won over the republicans "from step to step" without telling them where he was leading them. Neither in the Tunisian nor in the Tonkin affair did he explain the true situation to the legislative chambers. His behavior irritated parliament: the opposition, left and right, had reproached him many times for confronting the members of parliament with a *fait accompli* and for concealing the truth from them. Even his supporters were by degrees discouraged by his authoritarian behavior. The storm broke when an "accident" suddenly occurred of which parliament exaggerated the importance. This explanation is substantial: it rests on a close examination of the facts and the texts. But what would have happened if Jules Ferry had told parliament the truth?

In England and the United States the situation was far different: the English elections of 1895 had given a large majority to the Unionists, who had adopted imperialism. In the presidential elections of 1900, which carried Theodore Roosevelt to the vice-presidency, the candidate of the Democratic party, Bryan, had put the struggle against imperialism in the forefront of his campaign and had been clearly beaten. Neither Joseph Chamberlain nor Theodore Roosevelt encountered, then, difficulties comparable to those which arose in Italy and France. Nevertheless, they were obliged to maneuver. In the South African affair Chamberlain waited for public opinion to ripen before he acted. Still, he avoided summoning the House of Commons when he decided to resolve the crisis by force of arms: he started the war without consulting Parliament. Theodore Roosevelt ran against opposition in the Senate, whether it was a question of his policy in Santo Domingo or his moves in Panama. Even in these countries, where public opinion on the whole favored expansionist designs, statesmen had recourse to the method of the *fait accompli* because they perceived that parliamentary circles, when faced with reality, would hesitate to take action. . . .

THE ALLIANCE BETWEEN MOB
AND CAPITAL

HANNAH ARENDT

The first woman ever appointed a full professor at Princeton University, Hannah Arendt (1906–   ) was educated at Heidelberg under the philosopher Karl Jaspers and came to the United States in 1940 as a political refugee after residing for a number of years in France. In 1951 she published the much-discussed *The Origins of Totalitarianism* and in 1958 followed it with *The Human Condition*—both books involving the synthesis of history, philosophy, and political science. *The Origins of Totalitarianism* considers communism and fascism and their relations to nineteenth-century racialism and "imperialism."

"EXPANSION is everything," said Cecil Rhodes, and fell into despair, for every night he saw overhead "these stars . . . these vast worlds which we can never reach. I would annex the planets if I could." He had discovered the moving principle of the new, the imperialist era . . . and yet in a flash of wisdom Rhodes recognized at the same moment its inherent insanity and its contradiction to the human condition. Naturally, neither insight nor sadness changed his policies. He had no use for the flashes of wisdom that led him so far beyond the normal capacities of an ambitious businessman with a marked tendency toward megalomania.

"World politics is for a nation what megalomania is for an individual," said Eugen Richter (leader of the German progressive party) at about the same historical moment. But his opposition in the Reichstag to Bismarck's proposal to support private companies in the foundation of trading and maritime stations, showed clearly that he understood the economic needs of a nation in his time even less than Bismarck himself. It looked as though those who op-

posed or ignored imperialism – like Eugen Richter in Germany, or Gladstone in England, or Clemenceau in France – had lost touch with reality and did not realize that trade and economics had already involved every nation in world politics. The national principle was leading into provincial ignorance and the battle fought by sanity was lost.

Moderation and confusion were the only rewards of any stateman's consistent opposition to imperialist expansion. Thus Bismarck, in 1871, rejected the offer of French possessions in Africa in exchange for Alsace-Lorraine, and twenty years later acquired Heligoland from Great Britain in return for Uganda, Zanzibar, and Vitu – two kingdoms for a bathtub, as the German imperialists told him, not without justice. Thus in the eighties Clemenceau opposed the imperialist party in France when they wanted to send an expeditionary force to Egypt against the British, and thirty years later he surrendered the Mosul oil fields to England for the sake of a French-British alliance. Thus Gladstone was being denounced by Cromer in Egypt as "not a man

From Hannah Arendt, *The Origins of Totalitarianism*, Second Enlarged Edition (New York, 1958), pp. 124–125, 126–127, 147–148, 150–155. By permission of Hannah Arendt.

to whom the destinies of the British Empire could safely be entrusted."

That statesmen, who thought primarily in terms of the established national territory, were suspicious of imperialism was justified enough, except that more was involved than what they called "overseas adventures." They knew by instinct rather than by insight that this new expansion movement, in which "patriotism . . . is best expressed in money-making" (Huebbe-Schleiden) and the national flag is a "commercial asset" (Rhodes), could only destroy the political body of the nation-state. Conquest as well as empire building had fallen into disrepute for very good reasons. They had been carried out successfully only by governments which, like the Roman Republic, were based primarily on law, so that conquest could be followed by integration of the most heterogeneous peoples by imposing upon them a common law. The nation-state, however, based upon a homogeneous population's active consent to its government ("*le plébiscite de tous les jours*"), lacked such a unifying principle and would, in the case of conquest, have to assimilate rather than to integrate, to enforce consent rather than justice, that is, to degenerate into tryanny. Robespierre was already well aware of this when he exclaimed: "*Périssent les colonies si elles nous en coûtent l'honneur, la liberté.*"

Expansion as a permanent and supreme aim of politics is the central political idea of imperialism. Since it implies neither temporary looting nor the more lasting assimilation of conquest, it is an entirely new concept in the long history of political thought and action. The reason for this surprising originality — surprising because entirely new concepts are very rare in politics — is simply that this concept is not really political at all, but has its origin in the realm of business speculation, where expansion meant the permanent broadening of industrial production and economic transactions characteristic of the nineteenth century. . . .

In contrast to the economic structure, the political structure cannot be expanded indefinitely, because it is not based upon the productivity of man, which is, indeed, unlimited. Of all forms of government and organizations of people, the nation-state is least suited for unlimited growth because the genuine consent at its base cannot be stretched indefinitely, and is only rarely, and with difficulty, won from conquered peoples. No nation-state could with a clear conscience ever try to conquer foreign peoples, since such a conscience comes only from the conviction of the conquering nation that it is imposing a superior law upon barbarians. The nation, however, conceived of its law as an outgrowth of a unique national substance which was not valid beyond its own people and the boundaries of its own territory. . . .

* * *

When imperialism entered the scene of politics with the scramble for Africa in the eighties, it was promoted by businessmen, opposed fiercely by the governments in power, and welcomed by a surprisingly large section of the educated classes. To the last it seemed to be God-sent, a cure for all evils, an easy panacea for all conflicts. And it is true that imperialism in a sense did not disappoint these hopes. It gave a new lease on life to political and social structures which were quite obviously threatened by new social and political forces and which, under other circumstances, without the interference of imperialist developments, would hardly have needed two world wars to disappear.

As matters stood, imperialism spirited away all troubles and produced that deceptive feeling of security, so universal in pre-war Europe, which deceived all but the most sensitive minds. Péguy in France and Chesterton in England knew instinctively that they lived in a world of hollow pretense and that its stability was the greatest pretense of all. Until everything began to crumble, the stability of obviously outdated political structures was a fact, and their stubborn unconcerned longevity seemed to give the lie to those who felt the ground tremble under their feet. The solution of the riddle was imperialism. The answer to the fateful question: why did the European comity of nations allow this evil to spread until everything was destroyed, the good as well as the bad, is that all governments knew very well that their countries were secretly disintegrating, that the body politic was being destroyed from within, and that they lived on borrowed time.

Innocently enough, expansion appeared first as the outlet for excess capital production and offered a remedy, capital export. The tremendously increased wealth produced by capitalist production under a social system based on maldistribution had resulted in "oversaving"— that is, the accumulation of capital which was condemned to idleness within the existing national capacity for production and consumption. This money was actually superfluous, needed by nobody though owned by a growing class of somebodies. . . .

Older than the superfluous wealth was another by-product of capitalist production: the human debris that every crisis, following invariably upon each period of industrial growth, eliminated permanently from producing society. Men who had become permanently idle were as superfluous to the community as the owners of superfluous wealth. That they were an actual menace to society had been recognized throughout the nineteenth century and their export had helped to populate the dominions of Canada and Australia as well as the United States. The new fact in the imperialist era is that these two superfluous forces, superfluous capital and superfluous working power, joined hands and left the country together. The concept of expansion, the export of government power and annexation of every territory in which nationals had invested either their wealth or their work, seemed the only alternative to increasing losses in wealth and population. Imperialism and its idea of unlimited expansion seemed to offer a permanent remedy for a permanent evil.

Ironically enough, the first country in which superfluous wealth and superfluous men were brought together was itself becoming superfluous. South Africa had been in British possession since the beginning of the century because it assured the maritime road to India. The opening of the Suez Canal, however, and the subsequent administrative conquest of Egypt, lessened considerably the importance of the old trade station on the Cape. The British would, in all probability, have withdrawn from Africa just as all European nations had done whenever their possessions and trade interests in India were liquidated.

The particular irony and, in a sense, symbolical circumstance in the unexpected development of South Africa into the "culture-bed of Imperialism" lies in the very nature of its sudden attractiveness when it had lost all value for the Empire proper: diamond fields were discovered in the seventies and large gold mines in the eighties. The new desire for profit-at-any-price converged for the first time with the old fortune hunt. Prospectors, adventurers, and the scum of the big cities emigrated to the Dark Continent along with capital from industrially developed countries. From now on, the mob, begotten by the monstrous accumulation of capital, accompanied its begetter on those voyages of discovery where nothing was discovered but new possibilities for investment. The owners of superfluous wealth were the only men who could use the superfluous men who came from the four corners of the earth. Together they established the first paradise of parasites whose lifeblood was gold. Imperialism, the product of superfluous money and superfluous men, began its startling career by producing the most superfluous and unreal goods.

It may still be doubtful whether the panacea of expansion would have become so great a temptation for non-imperialists if it had offered its dangerous solutions only for those superfluous forces which, in any case, were already outside the nation's body corporate. The complicity of all parliamentary parties in imperialist programs is a matter of record. The history of the British Labor Party in this respect is an almost unbroken chain of justifications of Cecil Rhodes' early prediction: "The workmen find that although the Americans are exceedingly fond of them, and are just now exchanging the most brotherly sentiments with them yet are shutting out their goods. The workmen also find that Russia, France and Germany locally are doing the same, and the workmen see that if they do not look out they will have no place in the world to trade at all. And so the workmen have become Imperialist and the Liberal Party are following." In Germany, the liberals (and not the Conservative Party) were the actual promoters of that famous naval policy which contributed so heavily to the outbreak of the first World War. The Socialist Party wavered between active support of the imperialist naval policy (it repeatedly voted funds for the building of a German navy after 1906) and complete neglect of all questions of foreign policy. Occasional warnings against the *Lumpenproletariat*, and the possible bribing of sections of the working class with crumbs from the imperialist table, did not lead to a deeper understanding of the great appeal which the imperialist programs had to the rank and file of the party. In Marxist terms the new phenomenon of an alliance between mob and capital seemed so unnatural, so obviously in conflict with the doctrine of class struggle, that the actual dangers of the imperialist attempt — to divide mankind into master races and slave races, into higher and lower breeds, into colored peoples and white men, all of which were attempts to unify the people on the basis of the mob — were completely overlooked. Even the breakdown of international solidarity at the outbreak of the first World War did not disturb the complacency of the socialists and their faith in the proletariat as such. Socialists were still probing the economic laws of imperialism when imperialists had long since stopped obeying them, when in overseas countries these laws had been sacrificed to the "imperial factor" or to the "race factor," and when only a few elderly gentlemen in high finance still believed in the inalienable rights of the profit rate.

The curious weakness of popular opposition to imperialism, the numerous inconsistencies and outright broken promises of liberal statesmen, frequently ascribed to opportunism or bribery, have other and deeper causes. Neither opportunism nor bribery could have persuaded a man like Gladstone to break his promise, as the leader of the Liberal Party, to evacuate Egypt when he became Prime Minister. Half consciously and hardly articulately, these men shared with the people the conviction that the national body itself was so deeply split into classes, that class struggle was so universal a characteristic of modern political life, that the very cohesion of the nation was jeopardized. Expansion again appeared as a lifesaver, if and insofar as it could provide a common interest for the nation as a whole, and it is mainly for this reason that imperialists were allowed to become "parasites upon patriotism."

Partly, of course, such hopes still belonged with the old vicious practice of "healing" domestic conflicts with foreign adventures. The difference, however, is marked. Adventures are by their very nature limited in time and space; they may succeed temporarily in overcoming conflicts, although as a rule they fail and tend rather to sharpen them. From the very beginning the imperialist adventure of expansion appeared to be an eternal solution, because expansion was conceived as unlimited. Furthermore, imperialism was not an adventure in the usual sense, because it depended less on nationalist slogans than on the seemingly solid basis of economic interests. In a society of clashing interests, where the common good was identified with the sum total of individual interests, expansion as such appeared to be a possible common interest of the nation as a whole. Since the owning and dominant classes had convinced everybody that economic interest and the passion for ownership are a sound basis for the body politic, even non-imperialist statesmen were easily persuaded to yield when a common economic interest appeared on the horizon.

These then are the reasons why nationalism developed so clear a tendency toward imperialism, the inner contradiction of the two principles notwithstanding. The more ill-fitted nations were for the incorporation of foreign peoples (which contradicted the constitution of their own body politic), the more they were tempted to oppress them. In theory, there is an abyss between nationalism and imperialism; in practice, it can and has been bridged by tribal nationalism and outright racism. From the beginning, imperialists in all countries preached and boasted of their being "beyond the parties," and the only ones to speak for the nation as a whole. This was especially true of the Central and Eastern European countries with few or no overseas holdings; there the alliance between mob and capital took place at home and resented even more bitterly (and attacked much more violently) the national institutions and all national parties.

The contemptuous indifference of imperialist politicians to domestic issues was marked everywhere, however, and especially in England. While "parties above parties" like the Primrose League[1] were of secondary influence, imperialism was the chief cause of the degeneration of the two-party system into the Front Bench system, which led to a "diminution of the power of opposition" in Parliament and to a growth of "power of the Cabinet as against the House of Commons." Of course this was also carried through as a policy beyond the strife of parties and particular interests, and by men who claimed to speak for the nation as a whole. Such language was bound to attract and delude precisely those persons who still retained a spark of political idealism. The cry for unity resembled exactly

[1] An organization of conservatives dedicated to the principles of Disraeli, founded 1883. [Editor's note]

the battle cries which had always led peoples to war; and yet, nobody detected in the universal and permanent instrument of unity the germ of universal and permanent war.

Government officials engaged more actively than any other group in the nationalist brand of imperialism and were chiefly responsible for the confusion of imperialism with nationalism. The nation-states had created and depended upon the civil services as a permanent body of officials who served regardless of class interest and governmental changes. Their professional honor and self-respect — especially in England and Germany — derived from their being servants of the nation as a whole. They were the only group with a direct interest in supporting the state's fundamental claim to independence of classes and factions. That the authority of the nation-state itself depended largely on the economic independence and political neutrality of its civil servants becomes obvious in our time; the decline of nations has invariably started with the corruption of its permanent administration and the general conviction that civil servants are in the pay, not of the state, but of the owning classes. At the close of the century the owning classes had become so dominant that it was almost ridiculous for a state employee to keep up the pretense of serving the nation. Division into classes left them outside the social body and forced them to form a clique of their own. In the colonial services they escaped the actual disintegration of the national body. In ruling foreign peoples in faraway countries, they could much better pretend to be heroic servants of the nation, "who by their services had glorified the British race," than if they had stayed at home. The colonies were no longer simply "a vast system of outdoor relief for the upper classes" as James Mill could still describe them; they were to become the very backbone of British nationalism, which discovered in the domination of distant countries and the rule over strange peoples the only way to serve British, and nothing but

British, interests. The services actually believed that "the peculiar genius of each
nation shows itself nowhere more clearly
than in their system of dealing with subject
races."

The truth was that only far from home
could a citizen of England, Germany, or
France be nothing but an Englishman or
German or Frenchman. In his own country he was so entangled in economic interests or social loyalties that he felt closer to
a member of his class in a foreign country
than to a man of another class in his own.
Expansion gave nationalism a new lease on
life and therefore was accepted as an instrument of national politics. The members of
the new colonial societies and imperialist
leagues felt "far removed from the strife of
parties," and the farther away they moved
the stronger their belief that they "represented only a national purpose." This
shows the desperate state of the European
nations before imperialism, how fragile
their institutions had become, how outdated their social system proved in the face
of man's growing capacity to produce. The
means for preservation were desperate too,
and in the end the remedy proved worse

than the evil — which, incidentally, it did
not cure.

The alliance between capital and mob is
to be found at the genesis of every consistently imperialist policy. In some countries,
particularly in Great Britain, this new alliance between the much-too-rich and the
much-too-poor was and remained confined
to overseas possessions. The so-called hypocrisy of British policies was the result of
the good sense of English statesmen who
drew a sharp line between colonial methods
and normal domestic policies, thereby
avoiding with considerable success the
feared boomerang effect of imperialism
upon the homeland. In other countries,
particularly in Germany and Austria, the
alliance took effect at home in the form
of pan-movements, and to a lesser extent
in France, in a so-called colonial policy.
The aim of these "movements" was, so to
speak, to imperialize the whole nation (and
not only the "superfluous" part of it), to
combine domestic and foreign policy in
such a way as to organize the nation for
the looting of foreign territories and the
permanent degradation of alien peoples.

SUGGESTIONS FOR ADDITIONAL READING

While the bibliography dealing with various aspects of European expansion in the late nineteenth century is enormous, the number of works giving a broad, general coverage of the period as a whole is itself very small. Parker T. Moon's *Imperialism and World Politics* (New York, 1926) and Mary E. Townsend's and Cyrus H. Peake's *European Colonial Expansion since 1871* (Philadelphia, 1941) give standard accounts of European activities overseas from the late nineteenth century through the first part of the twentieth. George Hardy's *La Politique coloniale et le partage de la terre aux XIXe et XXe siècles* (Paris, 1937) covers the earlier part of the nineteenth century as well and adds a stimulating if complex interpretation which considers European expansion as somewhat analogous to the innate need of all organisms to expand.

For bibliographical purposes, works which analyze various interpretations of the period are helpful and numerous, although some are seriously colored by a particular point of view. The most useful of these general analyses is E. M. Winslow, *The Pattern of Imperialism* (New York, 1948), which offers a very detailed and quite technical study of economic and non-economic views and which itself tends to favor Schumpeter's line of thought. A straightforward comment on three eminent thinkers is Daniel H. Kruger, "Hobson, Lenin, and Schumpeter on Imperialism," *Journal of the History of Ideas*, XVI (April, 1955), 252–59. Brynjolf J. Hovde, "Socialistic Theories of Imperialism Prior to the Great War," *The Journal of Political Economy*, XXXVI (October, 1928), 569–91, is a clear summary. Horace B. Davis, "Conservative Writers on Imperialism," *Science and Society*, XVIII (Fall, 1954), 310–25, is violently critical of all non-economic interpretations. Although limited in scope, these works are probably more useful as

sources of bibliography than the bare and by now out-of-date, if comprehensive, list of Lowell J. Ragatz: *The Literature of European Imperialism, 1815–1939, A Bibliography* (Washington, 1944). In general, many of the volumes listed below have quite extensive bibliographies.

The protagonists of the theoretical debate over the nature of European expansion have generally been those espousing an economic interpretation. Perhaps the two most significant views from a theoretical point of view, besides Hobson's and Lenin's, are to be found in Rudolph Hilferding's *Das Finanzkapital* . . . (Vienna, 1910), which connects expansion with capitalism's financial troubles, and Rosa Luxemburg's *Die Akkumulation des Kapitals* . . . (Berlin, 1913), which holds to the capitalists' need for markets. One may find commentaries on and modifications of "Marxist" interpretations, either written in or translated into English, in: Nikolai Bukharin, *Imperialism and World Economy* (New York, 1929); Maurice Dobb, *Political Economy and Capitalism. Some Essays in Economic Tradition* (London, 1937), which in the relevant essay concentrates on the similarities and internal contradictions of mercantilism and imperialism; Paul M. Sweezy, *The Theory of Capitalist Development. Principles of Marxian Political Economy* (New York, 1942), which defends Lenin on imperialism; and Fritz Sternberg, *The Coming Crisis*, E. Fitzgerald, trans., (New York, 1947), which has a brief passage reflecting Sternberg's larger German study of 1926.

Among those works which include criticism of the economic interpretations of imperialism are Raymond Aron, "The Leninist Myth of Imperialism," *Partisan Review*, XVIII (November–December, 1951), 646–62 (later included in his book, *A Century of Total War*, New York, 1954); Franz Borkenau, *Socialism, National or Interna-*

tional (London, 1942), which approaches imperialism from the point of view of the labor movement; Hans J. Morgenthau, *Politics Among Nations. The Struggle for Power and Peace,* 3rd edition (New York, 1960), giving an interpretation organized around struggles for power; and Lionel Robbins, *The Economic Causes of War* (London, 1939), which attacks the economic theory of imperialism very clearly, especially in the relation of imperialism to war. On the same line as Robbins, Walter Sulzbach's *"Capitalistic Warmongers." A Modern Superstition* (Chicago, 1942), though brief, is stimulating. In *International Economics* (Glencoe, Ill., 1951), the economist Jacob Viner devotes a number of pages to a criticism of the economic interpretation; and Jacques Freymond's *Lenine et l'imperialisme* (Lausanne, 1951) is entirely devoted to it. Eduard Heimann, "Schumpeter and the Problems of Imperialism," *Social Research. An International Quarterly of Political and Social Science,* XIX (June, 1952), 177–97, is generally sympathetic to Schumpeter (it is this essay which Murray Greene answers in the text, above); while Schumpeter himself, in *Capitalism, Socialism, and Democracy,* 2nd edition (New York, 1942), pp. 49–54, devotes a few very trenchant pages to a criticism of the neo-Marxian view.

Works of a general nature which have a substantial orientation toward specific details rather than theory include, in economic interpretations, Leonard Woolf's *Economic Imperialism* (London, 1921); Nathaniel Peffer's *The White Man's Dilemma. Climax of the Age of Imperialism* (New York, 1927); and M. J. Bonn's *The Crumbling of Empire. The Disintegration of World Economy* (London, 1938) — all rather popular accounts for laymen. Grover Clark's well-known *A Place in the Sun* (New York, 1936) and *The Balance Sheets of Imperialism* . . . (New York, 1936) are more concerned with the effect or value of colonies than with their acquisition.

More detailed views of the period are often the result of considerable historical research. Considering the period from the point of view of the relations between European states, William L. Langer's *European Alliances and Alignments, 1871–1890* (New York, 1931) and *The Diplomacy of Imperialism, 1890–1902,* 2 vols. (New York, 1935) are unmatched both in detail and in scholarly approach. The two works are further enhanced by (especially in the second editions) excellent, annotated bibliographies. Also orientated diplomatically are Walter Lippmann, *The Stakes of Diplomacy* (New York, 1915), and A. J. P. Taylor, *Germany's First Bid for Colonies, 1884–1885,* (London, 1938) — both of which contain short sections on the problem in general.

Individuals concerned with European expansion have been analyzed in many works. Joseph Chamberlain, Cecil Rhodes, Lyautey, Jules Ferry, Leopold II, Francesco Crispi, Bismarck, and others have all been the subject of two or more biographies apiece. Two convenient, though occasionally superficial, collections of biographies — each with a detailed bibliography — are the French works, in the *Colonies et empires* series directed by C. A. Julien: #1, *Les Techniciens de la colonisation* . . . (Paris, 1947) and #5, *Les Politiques d'expansion impérialiste* (Paris, 1949), which include essays on all the individuals mentioned above except Bismarck. A rare but convenient summary of the views of many men may be found in Fred L. Hadsel, *Imperialism in the Views and Policies of Leading European Statesmen, 1875–1890* (Chicago, 1945), a brief Ph.D. thesis excerpt.

Germany has been treated in English in Mary E. Townsend's *The Rise and Fall of Germany's Colonial Empire, 1884–1918* (New York, 1930), a long and careful analysis of Germany's colonial experience. One should, however, be careful to read Professor Townsend's essay in "The Economic Impact of Imperial Germany," *The Journal of Economic History,* Supplemental Issue (December, 1943), 124–34, which suggests a different point of view about the beginnings of German expansion. Also relevant are William O. Aydelotte, *Bismarck and British Colonial Policy. The Problem of South West Africa, 1883–1885* (Philadelphia, 1937), and Harry R. Rudin, *Germans in the Cameroons, 1884–1914* . . . (New Haven, 1938), both of which devote some space to general matters. A readily accessible article is W. O. Henderson, "The German Colonial Empire, 1884–1918," *History*, XX (1935–1936), 151–58. A recent French survey, Henri Brunschwig, *L'Expansion allemande outre-mer du XVe siècle à nos jours* (Paris, 1957), is straightforward. One should also examine the various biographies of Bismarck — for example, Erich Eyck, *Bismarck and the German Empire* (London, 1950), pp. 272–81 — which attempt to analyze the forces which led to Bismarck's change of policy.

French activity has been considered in English in Thomas F. Power, Jr., *Jules Ferry and the Renaissance of French Imperialism* (New York, 1944), a sober attempt to disprove economic motivation for Ferry; Herbert I. Priestley's standard *France Overseas. A Study of Modern Imperialism* (New York, 1938); the useful (and opinionated) Stephen H. Roberts, *History of French Colonial Policy, 1870–1925*, 2 vols. (London, 1929); and, to be published shortly, Raymond F. Betts, *Assimilation and Association in French Colonial Theory, 1890–1914* (New York, 1961).

On different aspects of British expansion there are countless works. Alfred L. Burt, *The Evolution of the British Empire and Commonwealth* . . . (Boston, 1956); James A. Williamson, *A Short History of British Expansion*, 4th edition, 2 vols. (London, 1956); and Paul Knaplund, *The British Empire, 1815–1939* (New York, 1941), are good general histories which cover the late nineteenth century in some detail. More specific information may be found in A. P. Thornton, *The Imperial Idea and Its Enemies* (London, 1959); C. A. Bodelson, *Studies in Mid-Victorian Imperialism* (London, 1924); and J. E. Tyler, *The*

Struggle for Imperial Unity, 1868–1895 (New York, 1938), the last of which discusses British attitudes primarily from the point of view of the already existing empire. The recent volume III of the *Cambridge History of the British Empire*, entitled *The Empire-Commonwealth, 1870–1919* (Cambridge, 1959), has an immense store of information. Philip Magnus, *Kitchener: Portrait of an Imperialist* (London, 1958), is useful. Esmé Wingfield-Stratford's long work, *The History of British Civilization*, 2 vols. (London, 1928), gives a most stimulating interpretation in its second volume. William L. Strauss, *Joseph Chamberlain and the Theory of Imperialism* (Washington, 1942), deserves mention because of its interesting association of Chamberlain with social Darwinism. Tingfu F. Tsiang, *Labor and Empire, A Study of the Reaction of British Labor . . . to British Imperialism Since 1880* (New York, 1923), considers an important aspect of the dispute over expansion. See also: Richard Pares, "The Economic Factors in the History of the Empire," *The Economic History Review*, VII (May, 1937), 119–44, and D. G. Creighton, "The Victorians and the Empire," *The Canadian Historical Review*, XIX (1938), 138–53.

Of the extensive literature on special areas, only a few books may be mentioned. For the partition of Africa see Sir Harry H. Johnston, *A History of the Colonization of Africa by Alien Races*, 2nd and enlarged ed., (Cambridge, 1913), and Sir Charles Lucas, *The Partition and Colonization of Africa* (Oxford, 1922), both old but serviceable volumes. Two excellent studies by Roland Oliver, *The Missionary Factor in East Africa* (London, 1952) and *Sir Harry Johnston and the Scramble for Africa* (London, 1957), illuminate European motivations in particular cases. Lois A. C. Raphael, *The Cape to Cairo Dream* . . . (New York, 1936), discusses a major British goal. And from these volumes one may turn to the specific histories of West, East, and South Africa. For late nineteenth-century European activities in the Far East and the Pacific, one may begin with Guy H. Scholefield, *The Pacific, Its Past and Future* (London, 1919); *The Cambridge History of the British Empire,* vol. V, *The Indian Empire, 1858–1918* (Cambridge, 1932); and Sir John T. Pratt, *The Expansion of Europe into the Far East* (London, 1947), as well as the standard texts on Far Eastern history.

Useful works of a miscellaneous nature include Richard Koebner, "The Concept of Economic Imperialism," *The Economic History Review,* ser. 2, II (1949), 1–29, which examines European thinking around the turn of the century; Lowell Ragatz,

"Must We Rewrite the History of Imperialism," *Historical Studies. Australia and New Zealand,* VI (November, 1953), 90–98; and Herbert Feis, *Europe the World's Banker, 1870–1914* (New Haven, 1930), which discusses in detail the direction and nature of European foreign investment.

Finally, readers interested in the subject should study original sources in order to get an idea of European attitudes at the time. This involves examination of the works of Kipling, Seeley, Dilke, Leroy-Beaulieu, Harmond, and others, as well as the writings and speeches of the various statesmen directly involved.